THE RUSSIAN SEARCH
FOR PEACE
February–October 1917

Rex A. Wade

THE RUSSIAN SEARCH
FOR PEACE
February–October 1917

Stanford University Press
Stanford, California
1969

Stanford University Press
Stanford, California
© 1969 by the Board of Trustees of the
Leland Stanford Junior University
Printed in the United States of America
SBN 8047-0707-3
LC 79-83120

PREFACE

The Russian revolution of 1917 took place in the third year of the Great War, a concurrence of events that posed certain problems for those who would lead the revolution. The focus of this book is on Russian revolutionary policies on foreign affairs and the war between the February and October revolutions, specifically on the dilemma embodied in the formulation "the revolution will kill the war, or the war will kill the revolution." The major concern is with the programs advanced by various groups and individuals, how those programs were or were not implemented, and how they affected the political fortunes of their proponents, rather than with the details of diplomatic negotiations and international relations. More particularly, the study concentrates on the leadership of the Petrograd Soviet after the February revolution and the leaders' struggle to evolve a peace program, to get it accepted as government policy, and to implement it internationally.

The Russian revolution traditionally has been studied primarily as the triumph of Bolshevism, the work of Lenin and Trotsky. When the light of historical and polemical writing has been turned from the Bolsheviks, it has usually focused on the dramatic and somewhat tragic figures of Kerensky and Miliukov, even though they often seem to have operated in a void, separated from the political movements and forces that determined the fate of the revolution. This study suggests that the Russian revolution is best studied and understood by concentrating on the moderates, here defined as the Menshevik–Socialist Revolutionary bloc that controlled the Petrograd Soviet of Workers' and Soldiers' Deputies, the All-Russian Congress of Soviets, and most local soviets after the February revolution. If there was a locus of power between February and

October, it was in the soviets, especially the Petrograd Soviet. The question posed, therefore, is not how the Bolsheviks seized power so much as how and why the moderates lost it. That is the question to which this work addresses itself. This study concludes that the issue of war and peace was crucial, the one area where the failure of the moderates was most catastrophic in its results; that failure more than any other led to October.

The author is indebted to many people and institutions for their help. Albin T. Anderson, of the University of Nebraska, guided my graduate studies and has encouraged me throughout the long process of transforming my dissertation into this book. Several people have provided encouragement and read parts or all of the manuscript at some point, notably Richard Debo, William Rosenberg, Robert Koehl, and Daniel Graf. Alexander Vucinich continually encouraged me during the final stages of writing. Ladis K. D. Kristof generously shared his knowledge of the Mensheviks and discussed several problems with me. Their suggestions have made a better book, though its faults remain my responsibility. Jess Bell and Barbara Mnookin have been all an author could wish in editors. Jan Larson and Joyce Richter ably and patiently typed the early drafts. My wife, Beryl, not only typed the final draft but assisted and encouraged me—frequently showing great forbearance—through all the phases of research and writing.

Numerous libraries made their materials available, and many librarians generously gave their help. First and foremost I must thank the Hoover Institution on War, Peace and Revolution for the use of its outstanding collection on the revolution and for providing work space during two lengthy visits. Mrs. Arline Paul, head of the Reference Department there, has provided valuable assistance over several years, and this author owes her a special debt of appreciation. I must also express special appreciation for the help of Anna Bourguina, curator of the Nicolaevsky Collection at the Hoover Institution, both for providing written materials and for sharing with me her rich store of knowledge about Tsereteli and his circle. Special thanks must go to the University of Nebraska library, and particularly Mrs. Jean Troutman, for help rendered when I was just beginning this study. I also wish to acknowledge the cooperation of the staff of the Archive of Russian and East European History and Culture, Columbia University, and those of the libraries of the University of Chicago, Hunter College (Bernstein Collection), the Missouri State Historical Society (David Francis papers), the University of Wisconsin, the University of Minnesota, the University of California, Berkeley, and Wisconsin State University, La Crosse.

Financial assistance in the form of a Summer Stipend from the National Endowment for the Humanities and a supplementary grant from the University of Hawaii provided the freedom from teaching duties necessary to finish this study. Wisconsin State University Board of Regents grants assisted the author in his earlier research.

The illustrations following page 68 are sketches made by Iu. K. Artsybushev at the Moscow State Conference of August 1917, and published in folio form under the title *12, 14, i 15 avgusta v Moskve; Risunki Iu. K. Artsybusheva na zasedaniiakh Gosudarstvennago soveshchaniia* (Moskva: D. Makovskii, 1917).

Transliteration is based on the Library of Congress system, but diacritical marks and the hard and soft signs are omitted. However, where names or terms have acquired a common usage in English, this usage has been retained: for example, Kerensky rather than Kerenskii, soviet rather than sovet. In 1917 Russia was still using the Julian, or Old Style, calendar, which was 13 days behind the Gregorian, or New Style, calendar used in the West. I have used the Old Style dates for events inside Russia. For treaties and international correspondence, and in other instances where it seemed desirable to indicate the Western date, both dates are given thus—September 2/15. Dates in Western newspapers are given thus—September 15(2). All dates are 1917 unless otherwise indicated.

R. A. W.

Contents

THE RUSSIAN SEARCH
FOR PEACE
February–October 1917

I

The February Revolution

Revolution broke out in Russia in the third year of the terribly destructive conflict known to its own generation as the Great War. This coincidence of war and revolution profoundly affected the course of both, but especially that of the revolution. In Russia, as in the other belligerent countries, the outbreak of the war in 1914 brought a sudden domestic political truce, as moderates committed to reform and some of the radicals committed to the destruction of the regime put aside politics to rally to the defense of the country. An ominous note was struck, however, by the fact that in Russia alone a large percentage, probably most, of the leading socialist and radical figures refused to support the war effort. Indeed, the political truce broke down more quickly in Russia than in the other belligerent countries. The old problems of the Russian Empire and the new tensions created by the war were so great that the upsurge of patriotism could only temporarily gloss them over. By 1917 a widespread disaffection covered the land, expressing itself in many ways. Anger over an economic privation worsened by the war was reflected in a rapid growth of the strike movement. Frustration over the inept prosecution of the war and over the deterioration of the government, which was dramatized by the rise of Rasputin, was evident in a growing hostility and bluntness in the Duma. Disaffection among the troops was apparent in a rapidly mounting rate of desertion. War-weariness grew rapidly among broad segments of the population. The main focus of dissatisfaction, whatever its origin or form of expression, was the war. By February of 1917, distaste for the war had crystallized opinion among all strata of society, leaving the regime without willing defenders.

The swelling tide of discontent suddenly erupted into revolution in late February. At first, there were simply disorders in food queues and a rash of strikes in factories in Petrograd, and it was not until February 27 that the seriousness of the situation became apparent. On that day, genuine revolution occurred in three quarters. First, some of the troops stationed in the city, most of them recent recruits, mutinied when they were ordered to suppress the disorders and instead joined the rebellious crowds in the streets. Other soldiers, including the traditionally reliable cossacks, declared themselves neutral. The government lost control of its main instrument of coercion, and the insurgents controlled the streets of the capital. This was revolution on the first and perhaps most critical level. It was, however, spontaneous and anarchic, and leadership was sorely needed if the revolution was to be permanently successful.

That leadership was provided by the actions taken in two other quarters the same day. One of these quarters was the Imperial Duma, which met to consider an order of prorogation that had come from the Tsar during the night. Despite a general dissatisfaction with the existing government, only a few members of the Duma could be considered revolutionaries; most of them were monarchists. With crowds milling outside, the Duma was forced to act to provide some kind of leadership for the masses in the streets, who had already launched the revolution. Yet the majority of its members were unable to bring themselves to disobey the royal order of dissolution. Their anguish is well summed up in the words of the Duma president, Michael Rodzianko, who, aware of the enormous consequences of their actions at that hour, plaintively protested: "I have no desire to revolt. I am not a rebel. I made no revolution and do not intend to make one. If it is here it is because they would not listen to us. But I am not a revolutionist."[1] After debating the entire afternoon and evening, the members compromised and at midnight established a Temporary Committee of the Duma to act in their name. The Duma then dissolved, thereby denying itself any major role in the events to come. The Temporary Committee immediately announced that it was assuming responsibility for governing the city and for forming a provisional government. Calling for calm, the committee announced it was sending commissars from the Duma membership to oversee the continued functioning of the various departments of the bureaucracy. Though this action was to seem timid in the light of later events, it was a radical step for men of such conservative and moderate views, uncertain as they were about the final success of the revolution, and probably played a critical role in guaranteeing the success of the revolution. This, then, was revolution in a second quarter.

The third quarter of revolution that day was the Petrograd Soviet of Workers' Deputies, a hastily organized body that also claimed to give direction to the rebels. About 2 P.M. on the 27th, a group of 30 or 40 socialist leaders gathered in the Tauride Palace, the Duma building, and re-established the Soviet, which had existed during the revolution of 1905. Among those present were N. S. Chkheidze and M. I. Skobelev, two Menshevik members of the Duma, and N. N. Sukhanov and Iu. M. Steklov, two independent radical Social Democrats who stood between the Mensheviks and Bolsheviks in outlook and who were to play important roles in the first days of the revolution. The gathered leaders organized a Temporary Committee of the Soviet of Workers' Deputies and issued a proclamation calling for factory workers and army units to send representatives to a meeting of the Soviet that same night. In answer to that call, about 250 delegates met and elected an Executive Committee, with Chkheidze, Skobelev, and another Duma member, Alexander Kerensky, a Trudovik, as a presidium.* Chkheidze was elected chairman of the Soviet. The next day the name of the organization was changed to the Petrograd Soviet of Workers' and Soldiers' Deputies, reflecting the sizable number of delegates that had been sent from various army units.

The Soviet plenum was completely dominated by the Execu-

---

* The Trudoviks (Toilers), who were moderate agrarian socialists, were a parliamentary offshoot of the Socialist Revolutionaries, the main agrarian socialist party.

tive Committee from the beginning, and that domination wavered only on a few occasions, most notably in September, when the Menshevik–Socialist Revolutionary coalition on the Committee lost control to the Bolsheviks. The decisions of the Executive Committee were usually final, the Soviet almost always automatically approving the proposals submitted to it. The Soviet, whose membership grew to slightly under 3,000 in March, was more a sounding board for the Executive Committee than a decision-making body. Most of the rank and file membership, the overwhelming majority of whom were Socialist Revolutionary peasant-soldiers and Menshevik workers, lacked any real political schooling or sophistication.

The Executive Committee, which grew steadily as new members were added and which had about 90 members at the end of March, was itself gradually preempted by its bureau, although it never lost all functioning ability, as the Soviet did. It was composed primarily of professional revolutionaries and intellectuals of socialist inclination. At first party lines were blurred and there was little partisan squabbling among the various socialist groups. The original leaders were mostly new or second-rank men, the main party leaders and theorists being in exile. In the first days of the revolution, the committee met almost around the clock, often with only a few members in attendance. The sessions were chaotic. The political situation was uncertain, and there were constant interruptions for "emergencies," including demands that Chkheidze or some other leader speak to army units, which had come to avow their support of the Soviet. In Sukhanov's words, the sessions were "not meetings, but a frenzied and exhausting obstacle race."[2]

Despite the confusion, the Executive Committee began to gather up the reins of authority. Commissions were appointed to deal with the food supply, the press, and the work stoppage in the factories, and to perform other quasi-governmental activities. The committee was especially active in preparing the city for an expected counterattack from Tsarist supporters. The initial support of the Petrograd garrison was reinforced when the famous Order No. 1 was issued at the insistence of the soldiers' delegates. It not only regulated the service conditions of the garrison troops but also provided that the commands of the Soviet were to be obeyed above those of the Duma committee. In effect the Soviet was claiming the right to control the army, at least in Petrograd, a claim that reveals the leaders' immediate understanding of the critical role the army would play in the success of the revolution and the future balance of political power.[3]

After protracted negotiations, the Soviet leaders joined the Temporary Committee of the Duma in forming a new provisional government. The very fact that the Duma committee had to negotiate was a recognition of the Soviet's power and influence in the capital. Chkheidze, Sukhanov, Steklov, and N. D. Sokolov, a Menshevik member of the Executive Committee, were hastily organized into a delegation to meet with the Duma committee, and the bargaining began shortly after midnight on the morning of March 2. The discussions centered on two questions: the composition of the provisional government and the government's initial statement of policy. The second issue was soon resolved. The Soviet delegation presented a list of minimum demands that were, for the most part, guarantees of civil liberties. These were quickly agreed on as the basis for the announcement to be made by the new government, in return for Soviet support. The final proclamation followed the Soviet proposal very closely.[4]

The matter of the composition of the new government was more difficult. The members of the Duma committee proposed a list of ministers, drawn primarily from the Duma. Two of the Soviet leaders who were also Duma members, Kerensky and Chkheidze, were included in an effort to ensure the support of the Soviet and the socialist parties for the government. However, the Soviet leaders had already persuaded their followers to vote against participation in the government by Soviet members. Their rather strong feelings on this issue were based on a number of practical and theoretical concerns. In the first place, most of them adhered to a theory of revolutionary development that saw the current stage as a bourgeois, not a socialist, revolution, calling for a purely bourgeois government without socialist participation. More practically, most of them felt that they simply did not have the strength and administrative experience to establish a purely socialist government. Another consideration was the war. Many of the Soviet leaders believed that, as socialists, they could not join a government committed to the continuation of the war, as this government would be. On the other hand, they felt that if they were to take power and try to end the war immediately, their government would collapse under the strain of demobilization, lack of administrative experience, and opposition from pro-war groups. In addition, there was a psychological factor involved: these men had spent their lives in opposition to the government; the habit was not easily shed. There seems to have been an instinctive, emotional reaction to the idea of becoming government ministers and a strong preference for remaining "the opposition."[5] About 6 or 7 A.M. the weary members of the two committees dispersed without resolving the problem.

At a meeting of the Soviet the same afternoon, March 2, the Executive Committee secured approval for its negotiations with the Duma committee to that point and for its stand against the entry of Soviet members into the government. However, in the midst of the discussions, Kerensky burst into the hall and interrupted the proceedings with an impassioned appeal that the delegates show their faith in him by allowing him to accept the office of Minister of Justice. He received a rousing ovation, which he accepted as approval for his entry into the government, despite a formal vote shortly afterwards against members of the Soviet joining the government.[6] This episode, which well illustrates the chaotic and exuberant nature of Soviet meetings in those first days, resulted in an awkward situation in which a prominent Soviet member joined the government as an individual against the Soviet's stated position. However disconcerting this was to the leaders of the Executive Committee, they did not dare expel or discipline Kerensky for openly flouting their decisions, for he was the darling of the street crowds. Kerensky was thus in the very important and advantageous position of being the only man in both the government and the Executive Committee during the first two months of the revolution. This position did not bring him the power it might have, however, for he soon ceased to play an active role in the affairs of the Soviet, and so did not exercise much direct influence on its policies. Still, he was able to pose as the sole spokesman of "the revolutionary democracy" in the government, a stance that was not without value to him.

On the evening of March 2 the two committees met again and finally agreed on the composition of the new government. Its members were drawn mainly from the moderate and liberal wings of the Duma, but with the almost total disappearance of the monarchist and conservative elements from the scene and the rapid upsurge of the socialist parties, they now found themselves in the unexpected and uncomfortable position of being the "conservatives" of the new political spectrum. Yesterday's liberals had suddenly become today's conservatives. Most of them felt that the main work of the revolution had been accomplished by the overthrow of the Tsar, and that what remained was to consolidate the gains already made. They took a very restrictive view of the authority of the Provisional Government. As the name implies, they regarded the new government as a transitory regime whose primary duty was to hold the country intact until authority could be handed over to a government established by a constituent assembly, elections to which would be one of their prime responsibilities. Such a legalistic view was morally commendable, but not entirely practical in a revolutionary setting.

Though the Provisional Government was formed on the basis of the relatively conservative list drawn up by the Duma committee, its first policy statement was based on a draft written by the Soviet leaders, men who certainly did not feel that the revolution had already run its course. The first set of demands was quite moderate and entirely acceptable to the Duma leaders, but there were indications of future problems in the attitude of the Soviet Executive Committee, which, rejecting formal responsibility, still claimed the right of veto over government actions and the right to demand that certain policies be followed. This conditional and qualified support weakened the Provisional Government, already in extreme difficulty because of the Soviet's influence over the soldiers, workers, and peasants throughout Russia and especially in the capital. The real locus of power and authority, to the extent that one existed after February, lay in the Soviet. This was the origin of the famous *dvoevlastie*–the dual authority of a formal government with responsibility but little power, and an unofficial body with power but little official responsibility. This institutional cleavage spread throughout the country. It was reinforced by an intellectual cleavage between socialists and non-socialists, a we-they frame of mind that was especially strong among the Soviet leaders, who could not shake their traditional class struggle pattern of thought and mistrust of the bourgeoisie. This problem, never solved, contributed greatly to the inability of the moderate socialist and non-socialist groups to work together to create an effective government in 1917.

THE CLASH OF POLICIES

The Provisional Government's first program, announced on March 2, was limited to guarantees of civil liberties and a promise to convene a constituent assembly. There was no mention of foreign affairs. However, the government could not long avoid making a more comprehensive statement on its attitude toward the wide range of problems before it; most important, it could not remain silent on the most pressing problem facing Russia—the war. A second declaration was published March 7. In it, the government outlined its program in greater detail, and in two brief paragraphs made its first public and official statements on the questions of war and foreign affairs:

> The Government believes that the spirit of lofty patriotism, manifested during the struggle of the people against the old regime, will also inspire our valiant soldiers on the field of battle. For its own part, the Government will make every effort to provide our army with everything necessary to bring the war to a victorious conclusion.
>
> The Government will sacredly observe the alliances which bind us to other powers and will unswervingly carry out the agreements entered into with the allies.[1]

It was plain from these two passages that no important deviations from the former line of foreign policy were planned, and that the war would be carried on as before.

The foreign policy statement clearly reflected the thinking of the new Foreign Minister, Paul Miliukov. Miliukov was the acknowledged leader of the Cadet Party, the main liberal party in Russia and the one to which most of the ministers belonged, officially or in spirit.* He was also the recognized leader of the

---

* Cadet is an abbreviation of the party's earlier official name, the Constitutional Democratic Party. By 1917 the party was officially called the Party of the People's Freedom. Though all three names are used in the literature of this period, Cadet is the most common name and the one used throughout this study.

Duma group that helped form the Provisional Government, and it was widely assumed he would play a dominant role in the government.* A historian and university professor, he had become increasingly involved in liberal politics around the turn of the century. This earned him two forced trips abroad, during which he became widely known in political circles in Europe and the United States. His reputation as a democrat and ardent friend and admirer of the Western democracies did much to reassure the Allies about the danger of a change in Russia's foreign policy. Miliukov himself felt that the revolution in no way affected the basic foreign policy interests of Russia. Indeed, both he and his party had become increasingly nationalistic in the prewar period, and by 1917 fully accepted the expansionist policy of the fallen Tsarist regime. Miliukov strongly favored retaining two basic features of that policy: Russia's continuation of the war on the side of Britain and France and her annexation of Constantinople and the Straits as a reward for her war efforts.[2]

Miliukov's explanation of the causes and the nature of the revolution was simple, but only partly accurate. The immediate cause of the revolution, he believed, was the inability of the old regime to prosecute the war effectively, a failing that had led to a loss of confidence on the part of the public and the army. Though this evaluation was basically sound, Miliukov fell into a ruinous error in drawing conclusions from it. He held that since inept prosecution of the war had caused the fall of the old regime, the primary task of the new government should be the vigorous and efficient conduct of the war to a final and decisive victory. He was confident that this goal could be achieved: not only would the new government be more competent than the old, it would generate popular enthusiasm and the will to

---

* Many contemporary observers testify to his self-confidence and assertiveness. This never left him, even in defeat. In 1925 he was asked by the American historian Frank A. Golder if he thought anybody could have saved the situation in the summer of 1917 (at which time he was no longer in the government). Says Golder: "He hesitated a bit and finally said that he could have. When I pushed him a little, he did not make it clear to me how" (Golder, "Letter").

win the war. As he wrote later, "We expected that an outbreak of patriotic enthusiasm on the part of the liberated population would give new courage for the sacrifices still to be made. I must admit that the memory of the Great French Revolution— the thought of Valmy, of Danton—encouraged some of us in that hope."[3] This was a dubious analogy, especially for a historian, and the error was to prove fatal for Miliukov's career. Baron Boris Nolde, a fellow Cadet and co-worker in the Foreign Ministry, later described Miliukov's view of the revolution as "one of the most naive self-deceptions of this period so rich in every kind of fiction."[4] If Miliukov's reasoning made sense to his friends, it certainly did not to the mass of the Russian people, who had long since lost their enthusiasm for the war, whatever the regime directing it.

However erroneous Miliukov's evaluation of the revolutionary situation proved to be, he pressed hard to implement his vision of Russia's proper foreign policy. At a press interview on March 9, he expanded on the brief foreign policy statement contained in the government's declaration. "In diplomacy," he said, "such a sharp revolution as in internal affairs is of course impossible." He stressed that the revolution had brought Russia into closer relations with the Allies: now Russia too was a democracy and could share in the ideals of Western Europe concerning the nature and goals of the war; when the Allies spoke of a war for justice and freedom, it was no longer necessary to make an exception for Russia. Free Russia, Miliukov declared, did not aim at world domination, as did her enemies: "Our goal is only the realization of our national tasks and desires, not world domination, and the freedom of the peoples of Austria-Hungary and the liquidation of the domination of Turkey, which is based exclusively on the principles of force."[5] Miliukov's view that the revolution did not affect foreign policy was reflected in the composition of the diplomatic corps; with few exceptions the old personnel was kept on in both the diplomatic service and the Foreign Ministry, despite the complaints of some revolutionaries.[6]

Miliukov's disclaimers of Russian ambitions notwithstanding, he was committed to carrying out the expansionist foreign policy of his predecessors and immediately took steps to secure the wartime treaties that had been concluded with the Allies. He was not especially concerned about the first of these, the Declaration of London, which had been signed August 23/September 5, 1914, and by which the Allies pledged not to conclude a separate peace. Nor did this particular treaty come under the fire of the socialists; they too rejected the idea of a separate peace. The treaties that Miliukov was determined to maintain, and the socialists just as determined to destroy, were those concerning the annexation of enemy territory, if and when the Allies won the war. In a series of notes and agreements during the war, Russia had obtained British, French, and Italian approval for the annexation of the Bosphorus, the Sea of Marmora, and the Dardanelles, along with a sizable amount of land on both the eastern and western coasts, including Constantinople. Russia was also to annex some islands that were considered necessary to the defense of this area. In return, Russia had agreed to permit those three powers to carve out their own spheres of influence in other parts of the Ottoman empire. There was another major agreement between Russia and France only (the other Allies were not informed): Russia was to have a free hand in redrawing her western borders, France was to have the same with respect to her eastern borders. This agreement had been signed only in February 1917.[7]

Miliukov, wishing to preserve Russia's right to annex the territory promised in these treaties, set out immediately after the revolution to assure the Allies that there would be no basic change in Russian foreign policy, and that, having nothing to fear from the revolution, they had no reason to revoke the treaties. As early as March 4 he sent a long telegram to all Russian representatives abroad for presentation to the Foreign Ministers of the countries to which they were accredited. In it, he heavily stressed that it was his belief the revolution had not changed Russia's war or foreign policies and the new government would "strictly observe the international obligations contracted by the old regime." To this general statement was added a further paragraph in the messages sent to the Allied governments, one which well sums up Miliukov's outlook:

Shoulder to shoulder with [our Allies] we shall fight our common foe to the end, unswervingly and indefatigably. The Government, of which I am a member, will devote all its energy to the achievement of victory and will make every effort to correct as rapidly as possible the errors of the past, which may have paralyzed up to now the enthusiasm and the spirit of sacrifice of the Russian people.[8]

This telegram was followed by another on March 8, this one directed to the Russian ambassadors in the major Allied countries. Referring to his earlier telegram and the government's expressed willingness to meet Russia's treaty obligations, Miliukov stated that it was desirable for the Allies to reciprocate and confirm their obligations under the existing treaties. He specifically mentioned the treaties that spelled out the compensation each power was to receive after the war.[9] Assurances were quickly forthcoming; Italy and Great Britain responded on the 10th, France on the 11th.[10] On March 11 Miliukov received further evidence that he could expect foreign relations to continue as before when France, Britain, and Italy all extended diplomatic recognition. After these exchanges Miliukov had every reason to believe that Constantinople and the Straits, seemingly within Russia's grasp, would not be lost because of the change of regimes, and that Russian foreign relations would continue in a traditional pattern.

These diplomatic successes, however, were threatened by developments within the capital, where Miliukov's "business as usual" attitude was not universally shared. There appears to have been some opposition within the cabinet, as witness Miliukov's statement to the French ambassador, Maurice Paléologue, to the effect that he was unable to get the government to include as strong a passage in its policy statement of March 7 as he was making on his own.[11] (Miliukov received little sympathy from the French ambassador, who seemed to have had an obsessive concern for strong public declarations of Russia's fidelity to the war effort.) More ominous was the opposition to Miliukov's policy from outside the government. This was perceived and expressed succinctly by the British military attaché, General Knox, who upon receiving Miliukov's assurances that Russia would fight till her last drop of blood, wrote in his diary: "I have no doubt that Miliukov would, but can he answer for Russia?"[12]

Knox's question was a most pertinent one, for real power did not rest with the Provisional Government but with the Petrograd Soviet. The Soviet exercised actual authority in Petrograd, both in the streets and in the barracks. Even in the provinces and at the front its authority and prestige, communicated through the local soviets, eclipsed that of the Provisional Government and the government's local officials. This reality was recognized by Minister of War Guchkov as early as March 13, when he frankly told a conference of high-ranking army commanders: "We do not have authority, but only the appearance of authority; the real power lies with the Soviet of the Workers' and Soldiers' Deputies."[13] Given this power relationship, Miliukov's ability to fulfill his pledges to the Allies was conditional on the Soviet's support. It quickly became apparent, however, that the Soviet had very definite ideas of its own on foreign policy, and that such support would not be forthcoming.

Once it was obvious that the revolution had succeeded, some of the Soviet leaders began to face up to the problem of adopting a position on the war. They found themselves split into the same two broad camps that had divided European socialism since the beginning of the war. In one camp were the "Defensists," who placed heavy emphasis on the need to defend the country and called for military victory over the foreign enemy. In the other were the antiwar socialists, variously known as "Internationalists," "Zimmerwaldists," and "Defeatists," who, for the most part, wanted the earliest possible end to the war and laid great emphasis on concerted international socialist action to achieve that goal. Most of the leaders of the Soviet in these early days adhered to the Internationalist camp, though even then there were serious differences among them. But whatever their differences, virtually all the socialists were united in their opposition to Miliukov's policy of unrelenting war to total victory.

The first efforts to formulate a Soviet policy on the war apparently were made quite early, as early in fact as March 3, when Chkheidze and Sukhanov, both basically Internationalist in outlook, discussed the idea of issuing an appeal to the European socialist parties and workers to unite in order to force a general peace. On March 8 the Executive Committee took up the matter; three days later the committee approved, with minor changes, a document drawn up by Sukhanov and Steklov.[14] This Appeal to the People of the World was presented to the Soviet on March 14. In introducing it, Steklov emphasized that "the significance of the Russian Revolution extends far beyond the boundaries of Russia." Now, he argued, it was the people, not the "gentlemen gold-plated diplomats," who would decide questions of both domestic and foreign policy, and they must assume responsibility for ending the bloodshed. "If we all join forces, the war can be brought to an end." Steklov was followed by Chkheidze, who attempted to reassure the still patriotic soldiers that the appeal was not intended as a surrender in the face of the German invaders; what they were proposing was that the Germans follow the Russian example and overthrow the Kaiser, so that a peace between peoples could be made.[15] The soldiers were not easily persuaded, and there was even some momentary fear they might turn the proposal down.[16] However, in the end they were convinced that the appeal did not threaten the security of Russia, and it was unanimously approved. The language of the resolution is worth noting, both because the document dramatically illustrates the differences in attitude between the Soviet and Miliukov and because it clearly reflects the fervor and faith that animated the Soviet. After some introductory remarks on the revolution, it read:

The Russian people now possess full political liberty. They can now assert their mighty power in the internal government of the country and in its foreign policy. And, appealing to all people who are being destroyed and ruined in the monstrous war, we announce that the time has come to start a decisive struggle against the grasping ambitions of the governments of all countries; the time has come for the people to take into their own hands the decision of the question of war or peace.

Conscious of its revolutionary power, the Russian democracy announces that it will, by every means, resist the policy of conquest of its ruling classes, and it calls upon the peoples of Europe for concerted, decisive action in favor of peace.

We are appealing to our brother-proletarians of the Austro-German Coalition, and first of all, to the German proletariat. . . .

We will firmly defend our own liberty from all reactionary attempts from within, as well as from without. The Russian revolution will not retreat before the bayonets of conquerors, and will not allow itself to be crushed by foreign military force. But we are calling to you: Throw off the yoke of your semi-autocratic rule, as the Russian people have shaken off the Tsar's autocracy; refuse to serve as an instrument of conquest and violence in the hands of kings, landowners, and bankers —and then by our own efforts, we will stop the horrible butchery, which is disgracing humanity and is beclouding the great days of the birth of Russian freedom.

Toilers of all countries: We hold out to you the hand of brotherhood across the mountains of our brothers' corpses, across rivers of innocent blood and tears, over the smoking ruins of cities and villages, over the wreckage of the treasuries of civilization; we appeal to you for the reestablishment and strengthening of international unity. In it is the pledge of our future victories and the complete liberation of humanity.

Proletarians of all countries, unite![17]

The considerable differences in the tone of this declaration and that of Miliukov's statements gave warning that a major conflict on foreign policy probably could not be avoided and, indeed, would not be long in coming. However, in commenting on the Soviet proclamation, the main non-Soviet newspapers, though deploring the pacifist and class-struggle overtones, either did not see the conflict in views on foreign policy, or, more likely, chose to ignore it and to emphasize instead the agreement on the defense of the country. The socialist press heatedly objected to this attempt to gloss over the difference of viewpoints. In an editorial entitled "Two Positions," *Izvestiia* stressed that there was a very real and basic difference between the government and the Soviet on questions of foreign policy and the war. One position, said *Izvestiia*, was that of the "bourgeois imperialist parties," and it warned that such a position, a policy of "war to a decisive victory" for the satisfaction of annexationist desires for Constantinople and other areas, would be firmly opposed by the Soviet.[18]

In the end, the elaboration of the Soviet peace policy was not to be carried out by the men of March 14. It was, instead, the work of a number of prominent socialists who returned from exile in March and April. The first group to play a decisive role in the events of 1917 were a number of Siberian exiles who returned shortly after the Soviet appeal of March 14. They quickly took over the direction of the Soviet—along with some of the already established figures—and their leader, Irakli Tsereteli, became the acknowledged leader of the Executive Committee until the rise of the Bolsheviks in September. These new men held the fate of the revolution in their hands, and they took a special interest in the peace issue, on which they had distinct and strong opinions.

Tsereteli played a major role in the revolution, and, in fact, was probably the most important figure in the ruling circles from his return in March until July or August. He was not as flamboyant as Kerensky or as well known to foreigners as Miliukov, and therefore has not attracted as much attention as either in Western writings. Nevertheless, those who were involved in Russian politics recognized his importance at the time, and have testified to his significance in their later writings.[19] Tsereteli was one of several natives of Georgia who played fateful roles in the history of twentieth-century Russia. Born to an aristocratic family, he had risen to prominence as the leader of the Social Democrats in the second Duma.[20] Upon the dissolution of the Duma in 1907 he was exiled to Siberia, where he remained until the revolution. Despite his youth—he was only thirty-five when he returned to Russia—Tsereteli was eminently qualified for a position of leadership. He was more adept at practical politics than most of the Menshevik–Socialist Revolutionary leaders, especially the older socialists like Victor Chernov and Iu. O. Martov, who were primarily theorists. At the same time, he was himself a capable theorist, an essential quality in a revolutionary movement emphasizing doctrinal correctness. Finally, he seems to have had the character and personality to inspire great trust and respect. A close associate later wrote that "his strength was not only in his exceptional oratorical ability . . . but also in clear and forceful political thinking and personal integrity that commanded respect even from his political enemies."[21] Even more important, Tsereteli "knew what he wanted, had a definite plan, believed firmly in it, and was able from the framework of this plan to examine and deal with particular issues that came up." These characteristics made him an effective leader in the confusion of 1917 and led men to follow him even in the face of their own doubts.[22] Another, less intimate, associate identified the same traits—integrity, conviction, and personal magnetism—as the ingredients that combined to make Tsereteli the leader of the Soviet in 1917, even in the fall, when the specific policies he advocated were failing and the Menshevik–Socialist Revolutionary coalition was reluctant to follow them any longer.[23]

Tsereteli's ability as a leader was clearly demonstrated in his organization of the movement known as Siberian Zimmerwaldism. The Siberian Zimmerwaldists were a small group of Russian socialists who, from Siberian exile, joined the great debate on the nature of the war and the correct socialist attitude toward it that swept European socialist circles in 1914. Gathered in and around Irkutsk, the most important figures were Tsereteli, Fedor Dan, who was a leading Menshevik, and Vladimir Voitinskii, a former Bolshevik who had turned toward Menshevism. The group also included a number of other Social Democrats who were to play active roles in 1917. These men established close ties with several Socialist Revolutionary leaders, most notably Abram Gots. In their writings, they joined the "Internationalists" in calling for the revival of the International and for a general peace; they thus came to share with them the name Zimmerwaldists (after the site of the antiwar socialist conference in 1915). The Siberians' goal was to reunify world socialism in the old International and, through it, to bring pressure on the warring governments to conclude a general peace based on socialist principles. This involved the twofold task of gathering popular support and of bringing the prowar socialists back to "true Internationalism," i.e., an antiwar position.

There were, however, important differences among the Zimmerwaldist groups. The Siberian Zimmerwaldists, for instance, made an effort to mobilize a broad spectrum of socialist opinion, and it was in Siberia that the groundwork was laid for the Menshevik–Socialist Revolutionary coalition that dominated the Petrograd Soviet in 1917. The most important difference, however, was the stand the Siberian group took on the war. Though they held to a firmly antiwar position, they were prepared to admit that under certain conditions the defense of one's country was justifiable. This theme was not well developed and went relatively unnoticed in their writings during the early war years, but when it was emphasized in 1917, it provided just the combination of national defense and Internationalism needed to construct the broad center position that most Russian socialists could and did accept. That position, which came to be called Revolutionary Defensism, was the basis on which the Siberian group gained ascendancy in the Soviet and, for a time, in the government.[24]

While en route to Petrograd from exile, the Siberian Zimmerwaldists read, with mixed feelings, the appeal of March 14. They found it and other Soviet statements basically sound, but lacking precision—vague statements of principle without any indication of how the desired goals might be achieved.[25] The Siberians believed they could provide the necessary clarity, and they wasted no time in attempting to do so. They arrived in Petrograd the morning of March 20, and that very evening Tsereteli had a chance to speak out. In an address to the Soldiers' Section of the Soviet, he first praised the soldiers for their actions thus far, and then went on to point out the need to unite the struggle for peace with the defense of the revolution against a foreign military threat.[26] Soon after, he unexpectedly found an even better opportunity to press his view. The occasion was a debate on a resolution concerning the regulation of the Soviet's foreign policy slogans, which was introduced in the Executive Committee by Sukhanov on March 21.

Word quickly spread that the Executive Committee meeting of March 21 would be an especially important one, and the meeting room was jammed with both members and spectators. Sukhanov, as the sponsor of the resolution, began what was to be a momentous debate. He stressed the need for the Soviet to begin a systematic nationwide campaign for peace and to mobilize the proletariat and garrisons of the capital in support of Soviet peace slogans. While putting his main emphasis on peace efforts, he tried to forestall criticism by arguing that such a campaign would not weaken the front; that, on the contrary, the morale of the army would be improved if the troops knew they were fighting for liberty instead of imperialist annexations. His effort did not satisfy Tsereteli, who had been co-opted to the committee immediately upon his arrival, and who now rose in the packed and expectant hall to make his maiden speech. Tsereteli felt Sukhanov's presentation of the problem had been too one-sided in its emphasis on a peace campaign and so made Defensism the central theme of his speech. He asserted that the revolution (i.e., the Soviet), in taking upon itself the necessary obligation of striving for peace, was also obliged to make certain that its accomplishments were not destroyed by foreign enemies. A peace policy therefore must be accompanied by measures to ensure the defense of the country and the revolution. Tsereteli appealed to the authority of Friedrich Engels and the prewar German Social Democratic leader August Bebel as approving the notion of "just defense." The Soviet must not follow a policy of irresponsible opposition, he argued, but a constructive policy of peace *and* defense.[27] Here, Tsereteli was attempting to strike a balance between the desire for peace and the need for defense, the balance that was at the heart of Siberian Zimmerwaldism, now transformed into Revolutionary Defensism.

This message was very different from what had been expected. The listeners were stunned, completely surprised that Tsereteli, a reputed antiwar Zimmerwaldist, should so heavily stress Defensism. To Tsereteli's own consternation, the Defensist wing of the Executive Committee picked up this theme and carried it even further. The rest of the meeting was spent in stormy debate.[28] When the meeting was resumed the next day, Tsereteli again surprised the Executive Committee. He had been startled by the way in which the Defensists had pounced on the theme of defense and ignored the peace issue completely. Therefore he laid a new resolution before the Executive Committee leaders, a statement that contained the balanced position he had intended in the first place. Sukhanov accepted the new resolution with only minor changes, and it was passed by the Executive Committee by an overwhelming majority.[29]

Proposals for implementation quickly followed. The more staunchly antiwar left wing proposed that the Soviet begin a general campaign against the foreign policy of the government. Tsereteli countered this suggestion by proposing that the Liaison Commission of the Executive Committee be instructed to inform the Provisional Government of the committee's point of view on peace and to demand an official repudiation of imperialist war aims.* The Executive Committee, he argued, could then undertake a peace campaign either against or with the government, depending on the official response. Tsereteli's resolution passed.[30] This proposal was typical of the approach he was to favor in the Soviet's relations with the Government: quiet negotiation and a reasoned settlement of conflicting views rather than cries for mass demonstrations and confrontation. Tsereteli's inclination to seek mutual agreement was not simply a matter of temperament; it also reflected the experience of the first days of the revolution in Irkutsk, when, as chairman of a Committee of Public Organizations, he had worked with bourgeois groups in governing the city.[31]

---

* The Liaison Commission had been established earlier to provide a formal setting for meetings between the Soviet leaders and government officials.

The meetings of March 21–22 mark an important point in the development of the leadership, policies, tactics, and organization of the Soviet, a point at which the era of rather spontaneous revolutionary leadership and policies ended and more fixed leadership took over. Indeed, the fluidity of Soviet leadership and policy was one reason the Tsereteli group was so readily able to assert itself; they appeared on the scene just as the need for a more precise policy line and greater organization was beginning to be felt. V. B. Stankevich, a prominent member of the Executive Committee from February to the Bolshevik seizure, later commented that the history of the Soviet and the Executive Committee could be divided into two periods: before and after Tsereteli's return. The first period, he said, was characterized by vagueness, vacillation, and disorganization, with each member attempting to use the name of the Executive Committee to support his own personal views and policies. In contrast, the second was a period in which Tsereteli organized the Executive Committee and the Soviet into efficient and disciplined organs under his own firm direction.[32]

The new leadership group within the Executive Committee immediately set about organizing itself. For support it drew on a center bloc of Mensheviks and Socialist Revolutionaries, a bloc that in turn relied primarily on the Soldiers' Section of the Soviet, which was overwhelmingly peasant and Socialist Revolutionary, and which served as a rubber stamp for Executive Committee decisions. The Tsereteli group quickly took complete control of the Executive Committee and of the Soviet newspaper Izvestiia. The influence of the independent (and more radical) Internationalists, such as Sukhanov and Steklov, declined, and the smaller factions on the left and right had less and less real voice in the running of the committee or the Soviet. The increasingly influential Tsereteli group soon took on a distinct identification: it was frequently referred to as the presidium group (or, by more hostile commentators and sometimes jokingly by its own members, as the Star Chamber). Apart from Tsereteli, its most prominent members were Chkheidze, Skobelev,

Fedor Dan, Abram Gots, and Voitinskii. Dan and Gots, noted for their work as party organizers before the revolution, took over that essential task. Dan's responsibility was keeping the Mensheviks in line behind Tsereteli's policies, Gots was made responsible for the Socialist Revolutionaries. Chkheidze, as chairman of both the Soviet and the Executive Committee, guided these institutions in the service of the leadership group. Skobelev, who later became a government minister, played the role of troubleshooter, specializing in calming unruly regiments and factories. In Voitinskii, the leadership group gained a member with considerable literary ability: he was most adept at rapidly writing vivid and persuasive articles and proclamations. He also undertook emergency missions to factories and barracks, before leaving to become a commissar at the front after July. It is worth noting that Gots, Dan, and Voitinskii had been in Siberia with Tsereteli, and that Chkheidze and Skobelev, like Tsereteli, were from the Caucasus and had risen to prominence as Menshevik Duma deputies from that region. Beyond this core some prominent members of the Executive Committee were associated with the presidium group, notably M. I. Liber (Lieber, Goldman), a particularly outspoken anti-Bolshevik and Defensist, and the Socialist Revolutionary leaders Victor Chernov and Vladimir Zenzinov; Chernov provided the luster of his name, Zenzinov organizational skills.

It is quite clear that the presidium group worked closely together. However, since they conducted their affairs in a highly informal and personal way, the actual mechanics of their procedures are difficult to trace. In this regard, Voitinskii is the best source. In contrast to other memoirists, who simply hint at the existence of some informal decision-making mechanism, he provides some details of its operation. He states that the Soviet leaders coordinated their work at conferences (*soveshchaniia*) held each morning in Skobelev's apartment, where Tsereteli was living. The meetings were completely private, with no formal organization, no minutes, no chairman. The group gathered at the beginning of each day to discuss the problems before them, make decisions, and work out a plan of action. They not only reached agreements on what ought to be done, but even drew up drafts of resolutions and declarations to be submitted to the Soviet. Tsereteli played the leading role in these meetings, with Dan as his second. Both were regular participants, as were the other main figures of the presidium group (Gots, Chkheidze, Skobelev, Voitinskii). Two other Siberian Zimmerwaldists attended regularly: V. A. Anisimov, a Menshevik member of the presidium of the Executive Committee and former Bolshevik member of the second Duma, who was probably also a member of the presidium group, and K. M. Ermolaev, a close friend of Tsereteli and member of the Menshevik central committee (Organization Committee of the Russian Social Democratic Labor Party, or RSDRP). Other leaders of the Soviet participated from time to time. According to Voitinskii, Liber, Chernov, S. L. Vainstein (a Menshevik Siberian Zimmerwaldist), and N. S. Rozhkov (an independent social democrat, also a Siberian Zimmerwaldist) were frequent participants. To these names, Tsereteli adds B. O. Bogdanov and K. A. Gvozdev, both Menshevik members of the Executive Committee, A. P. Peshekhonov, the leader of the Popular Socialists (moderate agrarian socialists), and N. D. Avksentev, the Socialist Revolutionary chairman of the All-Russian Soviet of Peasants' Deputies. Gvozdev, Peshekhonov, and Avksentev were representatives of the most moderate wing of the Soviet and later held ministerial posts in the Provisional Government.[33] Here then, in informal conversation in a private apartment, the basic decisions were taken that were to decide the fate of the revolution from the end of March to October. In April, Tsereteli attempted to provide a mechanism that would permit an official body to make some of these decisions when he proposed the creation of a bureau of the Executive Committee composed entirely of members of the majority point of view. A bureau was in fact created, but all political factions were represented in it. Consequently, the informal conferences remained essential for the leaders to work out their strategy.[34]

The Executive Committee sessions of March 21–22 represent the end of one period and the beginning of another in the history of the Soviet and of the Russian revolution. During the first three weeks of the revolution, the Soviet leaders had been occupied with developing a basic stance on the questions of war, peace, and foreign relations. Now the revolution was to enter another stage, a stage in which new Soviet leaders with a better defined policy and tactics were to pressure the government to adopt and implement their foreign policy program, a stage that was to last a little over a month and to end in the first major crisis of the Provisional Government, the disintegration of the cabinet, and a new triumph for Tsereteli and the Siberian Zimmerwaldists.

MILIUKOV VS. THE SOVIET

With the reorganization of the Soviet and the refinement of its policy and tactics, the ground was prepared for a major clash with the government. At the same time, Miliukov and the Provisional Government were under pressure from other quarters. Demands for a full-scale review and revision of foreign policy appeared with increasing frequency in the socialist press, while from within the cabinet Kerensky publicly pressed for action.[1] Miliukov's initial response to these attacks, made on March 23, was to label the "peace without annexations" formula advocated by the Soviet a "German formula that they endeavor to pass off as an international socialist one." He also reiterated his belief that Russia must annex Constantinople and the Straits.[2] His statement provoked a furor and was publicly repudiated by both Kerensky and Nikolai V. Nekrasov, an increasingly independent-minded member of the left wing of the Cadet Party and a close associate of Kerensky throughout 1917. Miliukov overcame the reaction inside the government only by threatening to resign and take the other Cadet members—except Nekrasov—with him.[3]

It was more difficult, however, to calm the angry reaction of the Soviet leaders. Miliukov's statement, a total rejection of the appeal of March 14, was regarded by Soviet leaders as a direct affront and a challenge. More specifically, it was a great threat to Tsereteli's hopes of gaining government acceptance of the Soviet's peace policy. On March 24 government leaders met with the Liaison Commission of the Executive Committee. Tsereteli, who was making his first appearance on the commission, was the main spokesman of the Soviet delegation. Though both sides agreed on the need to strengthen the front and the country's defenses, there was no agreement on the effect their respective foreign policy programs would have on defense efforts. The Soviet leaders argued that the defense of the country could be assured only by taking into consideration the popular desire for peace: the people must be assured that the war was not being prolonged by any attempt to annex foreign territory and that all further sacrifices were to be made solely for the purpose of defending the country until a general peace could be obtained. Tsereteli stressed that the government could best give this assurance—and thereby rally popular support—by openly repudiating the old imperialist war aims and by taking positive steps to bring about a general negotiated peace.[4] This was to be the basic thesis of the Soviet on the interrelation of foreign policy and the war effort.

The government was divided in its reaction. Miliukov flatly rejected the Soviet proposals, but some of the ministers, especially Nekrasov and Michael I. Tereshchenko, a young non-party liberal who was Minister of Finance, indicated a willingness to meet the Soviets part way. In the course of a lengthy debate a gradual consensus in favor of some sort of compromise seemed to develop among the government members, though without expressed agreement on how far they should go in trying to reach a settlement with the Soviet. The meeting ended with a government decision to give further consideration to the Soviet proposals and inform the Executive Committee of its determination.[5]

What happened in the government meetings is not clear or recorded, but apparently it was at this time that the so-called left bloc, a group that believed closer working relations with the Soviet leadership were necessary, was formed within the cabinet. Since this bloc could usually rally a majority, Miliukov found himself in the minority on questions in his own specialty of foreign affairs. He was now faced with the alternative of capitulating or resigning. His supporters argued that he should compromise, on the grounds that any concessions made now would not be binding at the peace table. One of them, Vladimir Nabokov, commented later: "I considered a little Machiavel-

lism possible here."[6] In the end, a carefully worded document
that straddled the issue was composed; it was to be released not
as a diplomatic note but in the less binding form of a statement
to the Russian people. This document was discussed on March
26 at a joint meeting of the government, the Liaison Commission, and the Temporary Committee of the Duma (which was
invited to participate by the government in the hope it would
serve as a counterbalance to the Liaison Commission). The Soviet representatives stated that the statement was not categor-
ical enough in renouncing all claims to foreign territory. This
time, however, the government backed Miliukov and refused
to go any further, evidently feeling that they had made enough
concessions to the Soviets. No agreement was reached, and the
meeting ended with both Miliukov and the Soviet leaders declaring that they had "mental reservations" about the document
as it stood.[7]

On the 27th the Executive Committee met to decide what to
do next, in view of the unsatisfactory nature of the document.
At this point the government sent a revised copy of the declaration. It was found to have five words (six in English translation)
added, vital ones from the Soviet viewpoint. To the passage
stating that "the purpose of free Russia is not domination over
other nations, or seizure of their national possessions," was added the phrase "or forcible occupation of foreign territories."
This was the more sweeping statement the Soviet leaders had
demanded, or at least close enough to it to satisfy them for the
moment. They felt that it clearly renounced all annexations.
The document was approved.[8] Here again, the circumstances
surrounding this change in the government position are not
clear; apparently Miliukov had been persuaded or forced to add
this further concession to avoid a rupture with the Soviet. The
important section of the declaration, which appeared in the
press on March 28, read as follows:

The defense of our own inheritance by every means, and the liberation of our country from the invading enemy, constitute the foremost
and most urgent task of our fighters, defending the nation's liberty.

Leaving to the will of the people, in close union with our Allies, the final solution of all problems connected with the World War and its conclusion, the Provisional Government considers it to be its right and its duty to declare at this time that the purpose of free Russia is not domination over other nations, or seizure of their national possessions, or forcible occupation of foreign territories, but the establishment of stable peace on the basis of the self-determination of peoples. The Russian people does not intend to increase its world power at the expense of other nations. It has no desire to enslave or degrade any one. In the name of the loftiest principles of justice, it has removed the shackles from the Polish people. But the Russian people will not permit their fatherland to emerge from this great struggle humiliated and sapped in its vital forces.

These principles will be made the basis of the foreign policy of the Provisional Government, which is unswervingly executing the will of the people and defending the rights of our fatherland, fully observing at the same time all obligations assumed towards our Allies.[9]

The compromise nature of the document is readily apparent. The second paragraph dwells on the renunciation of annexations and indemnities, points the Soviets wanted made, and the first and third emphasize defense and treaty obligations, Miliukov's theme. It should be noted that the opening clause of the second paragraph in essence nullified the rest of the document. Leaving "the final solution of all problems" arising out of the war "to the will of the people" was an obvious reference to the fact that, regardless of what the Provisional Government or the Soviet might decide at this point, a constituent assembly would ultimately have the final word on the type of peace Russia concluded. Nevertheless, the dispute was not unimportant, for the policies followed at this time could and would severely restrict the assembly's freedom of choice, and the really critical decisions might well be taken before it met. Moreover, more than the future line of Russian foreign policy was at issue: essentially, this was a major power struggle between the Soviet leaders and the non-socialist groups led by Miliukov, a struggle whose outcome would determine the groups and individuals that would direct the country in the crucial months ahead.

The declaration of March 27 was undoubtedly a victory for the Soviet; the government had been forced to incorporate some of the Soviet's ideas into an official public statement on foreign policy. Beyond that, it was a personal triumph for Tsereteli, whose tactics in dealing with the government had been vindicated. However, it immediately became apparent that the declaration alone was not going to satisfy the Soviet, that it was in fact considered only a first step. Indeed, some pro-Soviet papers openly proclaimed this, even as they hailed the victory.[10] The Soviet leaders themselves elaborated their position when the All-Russian Conference of Soviets of Workers' and Soldiers' Deputies convened on March 29. On that occasion, Tsereteli, acting for the Executive Committee, delivered a report to the conference that contained an important statement of policy. After describing in glowing terms the strength of the "revolutionary democracy" and reviewing its achievements in issuing the appeal of March 14 and in forcing the government to make the declaration of March 27, he outlined the next objectives of the Soviet in the area of foreign affairs. It was not enough, he argued, for the Russian government simply to renounce its own annexationist ambitions; it must persuade the Allied governments to join in that renunciation and in drawing up a general declaration of war aims along the lines of the Russian declaration.[11] This was to be a key element in the Soviet's foreign policy program down to the Bolshevik seizure of power.

These ideas were embodied in an Executive Committee resolution Tsereteli submitted to the conference at the end of his speech. Attempts were made to expand the demands on the government as presented in the resolution, notably by a Bolshevik delegate, Nogin, who offered an amendment calling for publication of the secret treaties, and by Liber, who proposed that a call for an international socialist conference be added. Tsereteli strongly opposed the first on the grounds that such action at this point might alienate not only the Allied governments but the Allied peoples as well, and rejected the second on the grounds that such a conference should be the subject of a separate resolution. His recent triumph made it virtually impossible to challenge his tactics at this time, and the attempts to make substantive changes in the resolution were beaten back;[12] as finally passed, it had only minor changes. The resolution emphasized the need for defense and stressed the same points that Tsereteli had made earlier in his speech. Of the March 27 declaration, it said:

The Russian democracy attaches tremendous significance to this action of the Provisional Government and views it as an important step toward the realization of democratic principles in the realm of foreign policy. The Soviets of Workers' and Soldiers' Deputies will give their most energetic support to all the steps that the Provisional Government takes in this direction, and appeals to all the peoples, in our Allies' countries as well as in the countries at war with Russia, to exert pressure on their governments to renounce their programs of conquest. At that same time, the peoples of both coalitions must insist that their [respective] governments persuade their allies to join in the renunciation of annexations and indemnities. On its part, the Executive Committee emphasizes the necessity for the Provisional Government to enter into negotiations with its allies for the purpose of working out a general agreement along the lines indicated.

The revolutionary people of Russia will persist in their efforts to bring about an early conclusion of peace on the basis of the brotherhood and equality of free peoples. An official renunciation of all programs of conquest on the part of all governments is a powerful means of terminating the war on such conditions.[13]

This resolution, which was much more explicit than the appeal of March 14, made it plain that the Soviet leaders were not satisfied with the declaration of March 27 in the form of a statement to the Russian people. Clearly, they were going to insist that it be issued as a diplomatic document and that the government actively seek a general revision of all war aims. Miliukov let it be known just as clearly that he would resist such a move. In fact, by his own actions he stoked the fire of opposition. He continued to talk openly of acquiring Constantinople and the Straits. For instance, to a correspondent of the *Manchester Guardian*, who inquired whether the declaration of March 27 meant the final renunciation of Russian ambitions in the Straits area, he replied that Russia "must insist on the right to close the Straits to foreign warships and this is not possible unless she possesses the Straits and fortifies them."[14] At the same time, he further aroused the ire of the Soviet by some of his other actions, notably when he sought to delay the return to Russia of the more outspokenly antiwar socialists and to have Nicholas II sent to a safe refuge abroad. The declaration of March 27 was a compromise, and the truce it brought was very fragile.

On or about March 29, the date the conference of Soviets was convened, the International Relations Department of the Executive Committee produced a remarkable document, a kind of position paper written by the de facto head of the department, V. N. Rozanov, that clearly indicates the thinking of the Soviet leaders on their relationship with the government on questions of foreign policy.* Rozanov contended that, although the democratic character of the revolution and the internal conditions of the country had forced the Provisional Government to set new war aims (declaration of March 27), the Foreign Minister and his staff refused to accept the changes, and that as a result there was great uncertainty about Russia's foreign policy. The Executive Committee, he continued, having decided on a policy of seeking peace through a union of international democratic strength, must take measures to ensure that Russian foreign policy was in line with this program. To this end, he proposed what was in essence a joint Soviet-government commission to determine and control foreign affairs. This body, which would

* The International Relations Department of the Executive Committee played an important role in the efforts to convene an international socialist conference at Stockholm. Originally created on March 20, the department was charged with a variety of duties relating to foreign affairs, but its main task was to keep a close eye on the activities of Miliukov and to counter his releases to the foreign press by sending press clippings and statements of Soviet policy abroad. (The first reference to it calls it the Information Department.) It eventually even established a mimeographed newssheet, the semiweekly *Bulletin of the Department of International Relations of the Soviet of Workers' and Soldiers' Deputies,* which it distributed in French, English, and German language editions to European socialist and labor groups. When the Soviet began to take a more active interest in convening an international socialist conference, the nature of the department changed and its work became oriented toward this goal. Its role and importance declined as the Stockholm Conference project began to collapse. For the instructions establishing the department, see Pokrovskii and Iakovlev, I (*Protokoly*), 65–66. See also the department's own summary of its work in Shliapnikov, IV, 331–33.

meet regularly, would not only keep the Soviet leaders fully acquainted with the activities of the Foreign Ministry, but would initiate policies. Especially, it would be concerned with working out concrete peace terms and the measures needed to implement them.[15] This suggestion, which was fully in line with Tsereteli's "contact commission" approach to Soviet-government relations, was never implemented, even though reverberations from it were found in Soviet resolutions as late as the end of April. Political events in Russia swept on at breakneck speed, and the Soviet leaders soon turned from simply controlling Miliukov to defeating him.

The campaign against Miliukov and his foreign policy was taken up by the socialist press immediately after the issuance of the declaration. The official Menshevik paper, *Rabochaia Gazeta,* asserted that Russia must take the initiative and carry on an energetic peace campaign, and that the government must play a key role by immediately opening negotiations with the Allies to work out a common peace platform similar to the policy advocated by the Russian revolutionary democracy.[16] The independent moderate socialist paper *Den*, lashing out at Miliukov as "Minister of Personal Opinion," insisted that Miliukov must bow to the opposition to his policies both in and outside the cabinet, and either accept the new view or resign.[17]

The anti-Miliukov campaign became even more intense after Lenin, Chernov, and a number of other important socialist leaders returned from abroad in early April. Lenin's return on April 3 marked the appearance on the extreme left of a group that was in total and uncompromising opposition to both the government and the Soviet moderate majority led by Tsereteli. On April 7 Lenin published the "April Theses," in which he announced his complete rejection of the policies of both groups. With respect to the Soviet majority, he wrote: "In our attitude towards the war ... not the slightest concession to 'revolutionary defensism' is permissible." As for the government, there would be "no support for the Provisional Government; the utter falsity of all its promises should be made clear, particularly of those relating to the renunciation of annexations."[18] Such an uncompromising stand boded ill for the government and the Soviet moderates, though at the time it seemed to make Lenin a relatively unimportant figure in Russian politics. In fact, Lenin's program was so extreme that even his own disciples in the Bolshevik party were embarrassed by it. *Pravda*, which printed the theses, found it necessary to follow up the next day with an editorial disclaimer by Kamenev to the effect that Comrade Lenin's views were not those of the Central Committee of the Bolshevik Party or the editors.[19] Some of the old Bolsheviks, such as Voitinskii, finally broke with the party after Lenin's return, when his unwillingness to compromise became clear, and some of those very close to the Bolsheviks, such as Sukhanov and O. A. Ermanskii, stayed out of the party because of his extremism and demand for party discipline.[20] Though Lenin's oversimplified program, which called for the immediate satisfaction of popular demands, soon made him and his party a rallying point for the discontented, in April neither he nor the Bolsheviks had much influence in national or Soviet affairs.

In Chernov's case, the situation was quite different. He was one of the founders of the Socialist Revolutionary Party and its titular head. Basically a theorist, he never played the dominant role in Soviet affairs that he might have as head of the largest party. While abroad he had adopted a Zimmerwaldist position on the war, but after his return on April 8 he moved close to the Siberian Zimmerwaldism of Tsereteli and his group, retaining, however, a reputation of being more militantly anti-war than the Soviet leaders. Though he was certainly associated with this inner circle, it is questionable whether he should be considered an intimate member. Upon his return, he plunged headlong into the debate on foreign affairs. He at once began an attack on Miliukov and his policy, both in the press and inside the Executive Committee. From the front pages of the Socialist Revolutionary paper *Delo Naroda*, he laid down a barrage against Miliukov, referring to him as "Miliukov-Dardannelski" and asserting that Miliukov would yield his position only to force. In a statement to the Executive Committee, Chernov reported that the declaration of March 27 had received scant attention abroad, and that Miliukov was trying to convince the foreign public the revolution would not bring any appreciable change in Russian foreign policy. It was inadmissible, he declared, for a Foreign Minister of revolutionary Russia to take such a position.[21]

Chernov's report made a deep impression on the Executive Committee, which decided to accept his proposal that they urge the government to present the declaration of March 27 to the Allies as a diplomatic note.[22] On April 11, in a meeting with the government arranged specifically for this purpose, Chernov set forth the Soviet's proposal and the arguments for it. Sukhanov reports that he spoke "interminably," working his way around the point in order to wear down any opposition and to find the line of least resistance.[23] Chernov emphasized that from his contacts in Western Europe he was certain the document would be well received, to which Miliukov replied that from his own contacts he was equally certain it would not. The government was unwilling to become involved in a conflict with the Soviet like that preceding the declaration of March 27, however, and the matter was quickly resolved when Miliukov capitulated and agreed to send an appropriate note to the Allies. Evidently, the details of the transmission of the declaration were not worked out at this time,[24] an oversight that led directly to the eruption of a full-scale crisis two days later. Before that crisis is examined, however, another development must be noted: the intervention of Allied socialist delegations into the strained relations between the government and the Soviet.

Just as the campaign against Miliukov was building up, the Soviet gained added support with the arrival in Petrograd of several delegations of Allied socialists. The existence of the Soviet and its evident influence had caused apprehension in Allied government circles, but after hopes that it would die away proved illusory, the Allies turned to the problem of gaining Soviet support for the war effort and the Allied cause. To this end, both the French and the British sent delegations to Russia, one made of up three Socialist Party members of the Chamber of Deputies, the other of three members of the Labour Party; all six were devoted to waging the war to a victorious conclusion.[25]

The two delegations arrived in Petrograd on April 1. They were given a cool reception by the Soviet. Their socialism was much milder than all but the extreme right wing of the Soviet, and they had been denounced in advance in messages from more militant groups in the West. The Bolsheviks taunted the British about Great Britain's oppression of colonial countries and asked the very embarrassing question that was in everyone's mind: why the delegations did not include representatives of the antiwar minority in the two countries. For their part, the Allied socialists made it perfectly clear that their goal was to convince the Russians of the need to fight on to complete victory. This hardly endeared them to the members of the Soviet, most of whom desired immediate peace or at least the beginning of peace negotiations. One French delegate, Marcel Cachin, described their reception to the French ambassador: "Instead of being received as friends we were put through a regular cross-examination."[26]

Despite the initial chill, both the Soviets and the Allied socialists recognized their importance to each other, and so settled down to a detailed exchange of viewpoints. As the talks progressed, the extent of the differences between them became apparent. They were able to agree on the Soviet formula of peace without annexations or indemnities and self-determination of peoples, but not on how to interpret that formula when applied to specifics. The Russians were quite vague about the formula's precise application, and were even unwilling to promise that they would insist on a plebiscite on the return of Alsace-Lorraine to France, if the issue appeared to block otherwise promising peace negotiations with Germany. There were other points of disagreement on interpreting the formula as well. Nevertheless, the Allied socialists were willing to accept it in principle and to support the Soviet in forcing the government to make it part of Russia's foreign policy.[27]

An even more authoritative Allied delegate arrived in the person of Albert Thomas, the French Socialist leader and Minister of Munitions, who relieved the aristocratic French ambassador, Paléologue, of his duties and thus became, as *ministre en mission*, the highest official French spokesman. His main assignment was to encourage the Russians to take a more active role in the war, hopefully in the form of an offensive.[28] Thomas immediately joined his compatriots in supporting Kerensky and the Soviet against Miliukov on the question of foreign policy, and in so doing undercut one of Miliukov's strongest arguments: that the adoption of the Soviet program would cause trouble with the Allies. Miliukov, an old and trusted friend, was in fact being written off by the Allies, who realized that his openly annexationist views were aggravating the situation in Petrograd. The British ambassador, George Buchanan, commented in his diary on April 17 that, while Miliukov's loss would be a pity, "he has so little influence with his colleagues that one never knows whether he will be able to give effect to what he says."[29] Miliukov himself considerably understated the case when he later observed, "I was often unable to get my decisions adopted by the Cabinet."[30]

The steadily growing tensions between Miliukov on the one hand and the Soviet, Kerensky, and the Allied socialists on the other came to a head when Kerensky forced events with a statement to the press on April 12. According to his own later account he told the reporters that the government "was *preparing to consider the question* of dispatching a note to the Allies, informing them of Russia's new war aims," as contained in the declaration of March 27.[31] Whether he was misquoted, as he later claimed, or whether he in fact made a stronger statement, the papers the next morning quoted an official source* as saying that the government "is *at present preparing a note*"

---

* The statement appeared in the papers as a short news item, without giving Kerensky's name as the source.

(italics mine).[32] Miliukov angrily demanded that Kerensky retract the statement. Since there had as yet been no discussion in the government on the proposed note, the cabinet rebuked Kerensky and published a denial, which appeared April 14.[33] This, in turn, provoked a terrible outcry in Soviet circles. The pro-Soviet papers denounced Miliukov and demanded that the declaration be sent to the Allies immediately.[34] The Executive Committee, which was discussing the question of whether to support a government effort to float a domestic loan, the so-called Liberty Loan, decided to make endorsement conditional on the dispatch of the desired diplomatic note.[35] Thomas intervened directly on the Soviet side, urging Miliukov to send the note.[36]

Miliukov gave in under the intense pressure brought against him. However, he insisted on being allowed to send a covering explanatory note, whose purpose, he privately admitted, was to "eliminate the possibility of interpreting the Declaration to our detriment."[37] His note was approved by the whole cabinet, including Kerensky, who, although he did dispute some passages, later wrote that it "should have satisfied the most violent critics of Miliukoff's 'imperialism.' "[38] It was sent to the Allies on April 18 and first appeared in the press on the morning of April 20. In his note, Miliukov had given the declaration a markedly one-sided interpretation by ignoring the sections that referred to the renunciation of annexations and indemnities and stressing those that emphasized national defense and fidelity to the alliance and treaties. The note stressed prosecution of the war to a "decisive victory" and full observation of all obligations to the Allies. It ended with a passage that especially offended the Soviets: "the leading democracies will find a way to establish those *guarantees and sanctions* which are required to prevent new bloody encounters in the future" (italics mine).[39] These terms sounded suspiciously like euphemisms for "annexations and indemnities."

The Soviet reaction to the note was immediate and violent. The Executive Committee had not been sent a copy until the evening of April 19, at the same time that it was released to the press. The Soviet leaders were shocked at its contents and declared the note unacceptable. Their reaction was the more bitter when they realized that Miliukov had sent the note on April 18, or May 1, new style, the international labor holiday on which the Soviet had held special celebrations. The timing was felt to be a calculated affront. The Executive Committee split sharply on the question of what action to take. The left wing called for street demonstrations and Miliukov's resignation, but Tsereteli rejected this proposal, preferring to try to settle the conflict through negotiation with the government. However, he could not muster support for a definite policy, so badly had the events shaken his authority, and no decision was reached. On April 20, the left wing tried to carry their view to the Soviet plenum, but again no formal decision was taken, although the Soviet leaders found that they still had basic support in the Soviet.[40] Chkheidze, in defending the moderates' stand, explained the leadership's viewpoint and strategy succinctly: one could deduce anything one wanted from the ambiguous note, and all that was necessary was to clarify it, so that the country and the Allies would know that "the government does not intend to agree to annexations, expropriations, and contributions."[41] This could best be done through negotiations between the government and the Soviet leadership.

While the Soviet debated, and despite the leaders' opposition to demonstrations, large numbers of people, both soldiers and civilians, poured into the streets, carrying signs demanding Miliukov's resignation and in some cases even an end to the war. Some of the garrison troops proposed to arrest the ministers. These protests reflected the growing belief that Miliukov's policies were blocking the Soviet's peace efforts and prolonging the war. The Executive Committee worked strenuously to pacify the soldiers and discourage armed demonstrations. They also had to restrain the commander of the Petrograd garrison, Gen. Lavr Kornilov, fearing his effort at a show of force in support of the government would spark bloody strife, even civil war.

Interestingly enough, though the Bolshevik party organization of Petrograd and some of the rank and file actively encouraged anti-government demonstrations, Lenin and the Bolshevik leaders hesitated to call their followers into the streets and did so only on July 21, toward the end of the crisis. It seems clear that, for the most part, the protests were spontaneous outbursts rather than party-organized, and the Soviet leaders were only partly successful in calming the masses. The anti-Miliukov demonstrations called forth pro-Miliukov demonstrations, and inevitably a number of clashes occurred.[42]

Against this backdrop of disorder, the government and the Soviet leaders labored to reach some sort of agreement. It was no easy task. On the morning of the 20th, Tsereteli met with Nekrasov and Prince Georgii E. Lvov, the Prime Minister, at Lvov's house. Tsereteli emphasized that the Executive Committee felt the crisis could be resolved only by the dispatch of a new note annulling the note of the 18th. He suggested that the resignation of Miliukov would also help pacify the Soviet, but neither Lvov nor Nekrasov was willing to entertain the idea, fearing that the consequence would be the resignation of all the Cadet ministers and the collapse of the government. Since Tsereteli no more than they considered the overturn of the government a desirable solution, he agreed to a joint meeting of the Provisional Government, the Executive Committee, and the Duma Committee (which the government still hoped could be revived as a counterbalance to the Soviet) to work out a solution.[43]

The meeting opened about ten o'clock the evening of the 20th and lasted until four the next morning. The Executive Committee decided to appoint ten speakers, in order to present all shades of opinion within the Soviet, including the Bolshevik position. The basic disagreement among the various Soviet factions was over how extensive and concrete to make the demands on the government.[44] By allowing the more radical members to present their position, the Soviet leaders gained a psychological advantage, for they could then present their own case as a middle-ground compromise between the left wing of the Soviet and Miliukov. Also, they could blackmail the government by implying that the left wing might become increasingly influential, if their moderate demands were not met.

The government tried to shift the discussion away from the note itself to the broader political picture. Lvov gave a speech on the dangers of disunity, and the government ministers presented reports on the situation in their various fields, stressing the deplorable state of affairs and the need for all elements to compromise their differences and work together. References to Miliukov's note were generally couched in terms of surprise at the reaction to it, the implication being that the Soviets were overly suspicious. Miliukov did not make a report, but limited himself to answering questions. According to Stankevich, he gave the impression of "a man who was finished."[45] The Foreign Minister argued that the note had been misunderstood: his only intention had been to squelch rumors current in the West that Russia was about to make a separate peace and withdraw from the war. He attempted to bolster his position by reading a recent telegram from the French Foreign Ministry stating that France did not favor a conference to revise Allied war aims. This attempt to imply that his stand was correct and the Soviet position on foreign policy unrealistic made little impression on the Soviets, since they contended that the Russian policy should be to try to persuade the Allies to agree to such a conference. Moreover, Thomas cut the ground from beneath Miliukov by disavowing the telegram on behalf of France.

Although the Soviet leaders kept trying to steer the debate back to the subject of Miliukov's note, the government maneuver of bringing in other subjects was partly successful in moderating Soviet demands. The Soviet leaders insisted that the government abandon slogans popularly associated with imperialism and annexations, and that it send another note making clear Russia's determination to work for a general renunciation of annexationist aims by all the Allies as a step toward a negotiated peace. They did not, however, demand any

specific steps toward an Allied conference for that purpose or
the resignation of Miliukov (though this was foreshadowed in
Tsereteli's charge that the Foreign Minister did not understand
the psychology of the times and of the masses). Only Chernov
raised the issue of resignation directly, suggesting that Miliukov's reputation as a scholar might better qualify him for the
post of Minister of Education: Constantinople was less contro-
versial as a subject in geography than as a topic of diplomacy.
Chernov's suggestion was ignored.*

In the end, Miliukov flatly rejected the idea of sending a new
note because of the bad impression he felt this would make
abroad. Tsereteli countered with a proposal that an explanation
of the disputed sections of the previous note acceptable to the
Soviet be published for domestic consumption and then forwarded to the Allies. Tsereteli and Nekrasov then withdrew
from the room and together prepared a draft. The government
approved it with minor changes, apparently over the objection
of Miliukov, and the Soviet approved the amended version,
despite the objections of the Bolsheviks and others.[46]

The explanation was published April 22. It announced that
misunderstandings had arisen over the note of April 18, which
needed clarification. References to decisive victory, it explained,
had in mind those passages of the declaration of March 27 that
talked of the necessity of defense against the invader, and by
guarantees and sanctions was meant "the limitations of arma-
ments, international tribunals, etc."[47] The explanation was
quite lame, but it was enough to paper over the crisis temporarily.

With the publication of the explanation, the street disorders rapidly came to an end, and the antagonists attempted to
assess the recent events and their significance. Miliukov, in an
interview in the *New York Times*, claimed a victory: "Our
policy remains unchanged. We have conceded nothing."[48] He

* Ironically, Miliukov had talked with Vladimir Nabokov as early as April
about resigning the Foreign Ministry and taking the education portfolio instead. See V. Nabokov, p. 62.

repeated this claim to the British ambassador and telegraphed it to the Allies as well.[49] Evidently he considered it a victory that the government had been able to get the issue passed off as a misunderstanding, conveniently overlooking the fact that the government had been forced to make concessions, even if only verbal, and that he had again been overruled by the cabinet in his own speciality of foreign affairs at the demand of the Soviet. Some of the cabinet members more realistically appraised the affair as having underlined the power of the Soviet and the weakness of the government.[50] For their part, the Soviet leaders and the socialist press hailed the explanation as a considerable victory.[51] Their claim that they had won this battle, and that, moreover, they were winning the entire war with the government on foreign policy appears to be justified. However, what they seemed to have missed in the flush of triumph was the ominous implication in the behavior of the soldiers and workers. The crisis had pitted the "spontaneous indignation" of the masses, as Voitinskii later put it, against the "reason" of the leaders.[52] Leaders who oppose caution to the unbridled passion of armed mobs, no matter how sound their arguments, are in an extremely precarious position. Just how precarious was the position of the Soviet leaders was soon to become apparent.

The April crisis, like the earlier disputes preceding the declaration of March 27 and the agreement to send the declaration as a diplomatic note, arose out of the basic conflict between Miliukov and the Soviet, a conflict in which one attempted to hold to the old foreign policy, and the other steadily increased its demands for a major revision of that policy. As in the earlier crises, a compromise had been found, but one based primarily on the Soviet position and demands. Like the previous agreements, it was not a final solution but an expedient designed to avert a complete rupture and a final showdown. The battle over the two rival foreign programs was to continue as the main issue in the struggle for political supremacy between the Soviet leaders and the old liberal and moderate elements represented by Miliukov.

The tensions and suspicions that permeated the relations between the government and the Soviet leaders could not be bridged by negotiation and compromises much longer. Clearly, the new principles of foreign policy could be effectively translated into practice only if Miliukov left his post and if members of the Executive Committee joined the government. Both sides were reluctant to make such a shift, but the pressure of events pushed them inexorably in this direction. The formal authority of the government and the effective power of the Soviet had to be meshed. Increasingly, popular opinion favored a "coalition government" that would bring Soviet leaders into responsible government posts and, hopefully, end the confusion inherent in the *dvoevlastie,* the two authorities.

The idea of coalition gained favor in all circles after the April crisis; it seems to have been especially popular in soldiers' organizations. On April 26 the government, now firmly controlled by the advocates of bringing some of the Soviet leaders into it, issued an appeal calculated to draw on this support. Outlining the problems facing the country, the government held up the specter of civil war and promised to continue "its efforts directed at expanding its composition by drawing into responsible government work representatives of those active creative forces of the country who have not previously taken direct... part in the government of the state."[53] The same day Kerensky* published an open letter calling for representatives of the "toiling democracy" to join in the governing of the state.[54] Immediately after, on April 27, Lvov sent Chkheidze a letter, asking him to bring the question of a coalition government before the Executive Committee.[55]

The letter caused confusion in the Soviet leadership, for it was badly divided on the issue. The Socialist Revolutionaries and the various right-wing agrarian socialist groups generally

* Chernov (*Great Revolution*, p. 205) claims he composed Kerensky's letter for him, a claim that Kerensky hotly denies (see the editor's note in Browder and Kerensky, III, 1251–52). If Chernov indeed wrote the letter or was even a party to it, such a method of pressuring the Soviet leaders probably did not improve his already frequently strained relations with them.

supported the idea,[56] whereas the Mensheviks, the other half of
the coalition making up the Soviet majority, found themselves
allied with the Bolsheviks and some left-wing Socialist Revolutionaries and independents in opposing it. The Mensheviks,
under increasing pressure from both the public and their Socialist Revolutionary colleagues, were in a difficult position. The
inner circle of the Executive Committee met privately at Skobelev's house to discuss the issue. Tsereteli led the opposition to
coalition, and his speech, as reconstructed in his memoirs, was
a compelling argument against coalition:

Experience has shown that the Soviet, without merging with the government, retains the greatest possible influence upon the most inflam-
mable section of the population.... So long as we maintain this
position, we shall be able not only to check the growth of extremist
tendencies in the masses, but also to exercise a real influence upon the
government in the direction of a democratization of its policies, since
the government and the middle classes which back it are greatly im-
pressed by the power of the Soviet. Should we, on the other hand, in
joining the government, arouse hopes in the masses which we might
be unable to fulfill, this would strengthen the extremist left-wing
trends. And to the extent that our hold upon the masses weakens our
influence on the Government will decline, regardless of the presence
of our representatives in the Cabinet. The discrepancy between the
policies of the government and the yearnings of the masses will increase and, instead of the consolidation of a democratic government,
the outcome of our step will be the strengthening of maximalist tendencies in the masses.[57]

Under Tsereteli's urging the Menshevik leaders stood firm in
their opposition to a coalition, which prompted the Socialist
Revolutionaries to make it clear that without the Mensheviks
they would not feel able to undertake the formation of a coalition government. They did not devise any effective counter to
the Kerensky and Lvov letters, however.

The Executive Committee debated the issue the night of
April 28, with the Socialist Revolutionaries and other populist
groups generally for coalition, the Social Democratic groups—
Bolshevik, Menshevik, and independents—generally against it.
The Siberian Zimmerwaldist group held together, with at least
Gots of the Socialist Revolutionaries voting with Tsereteli

rather than with his party. Coalition was defeated by a close vote, variously described as 24–22 and 23–22, with eight abstentions. A large number of members simply avoided the issue by not attending.[58]

The subjects of foreign policy and coalition government were widely aired in various forums in the next few days. During a meeting of the members of all four past State Dumas on April 27, a clash occurred between Tsereteli and V. V. Shulgin, a monarchist member of the Duma, that illustrates the attitude of the most conservative elements among those accepting the revolution. Referring to the limitations that had been placed on the government by the Soviet, Shulgin stated: "Of course it is not in the same position as the government of the old regime, which is imprisoned in the Peter and Paul Fortress, but I would say that it is, so to speak, under 'house arrest'!" He adopted a technique Miliukov had used in his famous speech of November 1916, asking of the activities of the Soviet: "Is this stupidity or is it treason?"[59]

Tsereteli defended the Soviet against the attacks of Shulgin and others. He denied that the Soviet by its actions was weakening the army and the country; on the contrary, without the support of the Soviet, the government would be far weaker. Moreover, the army could be strengthened only if the troops were assured, as the Soviet ideology of Revolutionary Defensism sought to do, that they no longer fought and bled for imperialist war aims. He concluded with a brief call for cooperation as an alternative to coalition:

The Provisional Government should continue on the road it has started, the road of agreement [with the democratic elements as represented by the Soviets], and it should even more firmly carry out democratic ideals in internal and foreign politics, and if it does so with all the strength of its authority, the democracy will support this revolutionary Provisional Government with all its weight. In this way, with the united strength of all the vital forces of the country, we will carry our revolution to its conclusion and perhaps spread it to the whole world.[60]

Two days later, on April 29, the Congress of Delegates of the Front, meeting in Petrograd, was addressed by leading government and Soviet spokesmen. After two pessimistic speeches on the state of the country, one by Guchkov and the other, surprisingly, by Kerensky ("I regret that I did not die two months ago. I would have died happy with the dream that the flame of a new life has been kindled in Russia"), Tsereteli won overwhelming support for the main tenets of Revolutionary Defensism: a general peace on the Soviet formula and continued defense of the country until such time as peace was achieved.[61]

The discussion of foreign policy and coalition government was abruptly interrupted by the sudden resignation of the Minister of War, Guchkov, an Octobrist and a conservative in the prevailing political climate. Guchkov, dismayed at the growing strength of the socialists, was dissatisfied with the course of the government and with affairs generally. According to his own account, his decision was precipitated by a cabinet meeting held in Miliukov's absence, at which the ministers seemed in general agreement that Miliukov must go, and that the socialists must be included in the cabinet.[62]

At this new turn of events, the Menshevik leaders were under even more pressure from their supporters to join the cabinet. Telegrams and delegations demanding coalition deluged them. Tsereteli later wrote: "Every day, every hour, it became more and more difficult to resist this campaign."[63] On May 1 Lvov informed Tsereteli that the government would again ask the Soviet leaders to join in a coalition, and that, if the proposal was rejected, the cabinet would resign, leaving the country without a government.[64] Overwhelmed, Tsereteli and his colleagues capitulated. On May 2, after an all-night debate, the Executive Committee reversed itself and voted 44 to 19 for participation. The "no" votes were registered by the Bolsheviks, four Socialist Revolutionaries, and three Menshevik-Internationalists.[65]

The Soviet Executive Committee and the government met that same day to work out the composition and program of the new government. Save for some stronger language to emphasize that Russia was not preparing a separate peace with Germany, which was put in at government insistence, the program agreed on was essentially the same as that proposed by the Soviet.[66] The result was the virtual adoption of the Soviet foreign policy. The pertinent sections read:

(1) In its foreign policy the Provisional Government, rejecting, in concert with all the people, all thought of a separate peace, adopts openly as its aim the reestablishment of a general peace which shall not tend toward either domination over other nations, or violent usurpation of their territories—a peace without annexations or indemnities, and based on the rights of nations to decide their own affairs.... The Provisional Government will take steps toward bringing about an agreement with the Allies on the basis of its declaration of March 27.

(2) Convinced that the defeat of Russia and her allies not only would be a source of the greatest calamities to the people, but would postpone or make impossible the conclusion of a world-wide peace on the basis indicated above, the Provisional Government believes firmly that the Russian revolutionary army will not permit the German troops to destroy our Western Allies and then throw themselves upon us with the full force of their arms.[67]

With the adoption of this program, Miliukov left the government. The Executive Committee delegates evidently insisted on his resignation from the Foreign Ministry as a prerequisite for the formation of a coalition cabinet, but not on his leaving the government altogether. The fear was that a demand for his complete ouster would lead the Cadets to resign in a body, a development that no one wanted: the Cadet Party was the only important non-socialist political party, and any "coalition" without the Cadets would be a farce. During the period May 2–5, while the negotiations on the new government were under way, the Cadets tried to convince Miliukov to stay in the government in another post, on the grounds that he would thus be able to influence, if not direct, foreign policy. He disagreed, fearing that by staying on in any capacity he would appear to be lending his support to a policy he in fact rejected. He therefore preferred to resign and move into open opposition. His resignation, without that of the other Cadets, was a great relief to the Soviet leaders.[68]

The post of Foreign Minister was quickly filled. Apart from a few Socialist Revolutionaries who wanted Chernov (he was,

however, completely unacceptable to the non-socialists, being
regarded as a "defeatist"), virtually all the negotiators felt that
the ministry should remain in the hands of a non-socialist. For
one thing, this would reassure both the Cadets and the Allies,
and for another, no prominent socialist was eager to chance
losing his popularity with the masses by assuming this difficult
and risk-laden post. Tereshchenko, a non-affiliated liberal, was
the ready choice of all. A millionaire and widely traveled, he was
of a background that would almost certainly reassure the Allies;
at the same time he was recommended to the Soviet leaders by
Kerensky and Nekrasov as an adherent of "democratic methods"
in foreign policy. Further, he had the negative advantage of not
having any enemies.[69] Five socialists joined Kerensky in the
cabinet; the most important were Chernov, Skobelev, and Tsereteli. Chernov, titular head of the largest agrarian party, took
the Ministry of Agriculture, Skobelev, a Menshevik and member of the Tsereteli group, became Minister of Labor. Tsereteli
was reluctant to enter the government, preferring to concentrate
on the direction of the Soviet. However, in the face of almost
universal insistence that he be in the cabinet, he accepted the
position of Minister of Post and Telegraph, an office that would
demand very little of his time. There was also another important change: Kerensky became Minister of War. Lvov remained
Prime Minister.

The two leading figures of the new government were Kerensky and Tsereteli. As for the party composition of the cabinet,
on the one hand were the six socialist ministers, though Kerensky was in the process of shaking off his direct ties with the
Soviet. On the other were five Cadets, though Nekrasov had become increasingly independent and was soon to break party
bonds. In the middle were four non-socialists who either had
no party affiliation or were from parties that had ceased to have
any importance or even to exist. Since some of the non-socialists
and Nekrasov could be counted on to vote with the Soviet representatives on most issues, they seemed in a position to dominate the cabinet. This domination was not secure, however, for

a more meaningful breakdown of the power relationship shows the cabinet membership in quite another light: the five new Soviet representatives led by Tsereteli and Chernov, the four Cadets (minus Nekrasov), and a third group centered around Kerensky composed of Tereshchenko, Nekrasov, and often Prince Lvov and the two remaining non-party ministers.* Viewed this way, the control of the cabinet depended on cooperation between the Tsereteli and Kerensky groups. The reality of their power base made the Soviet leaders the dominant element of the government; without their approval no policy could be initiated. Still, Kerensky's great personal prestige and growing vanity made the alliance precarious. For a time, however, the objectives of the two groups were in harmony, especially with respect to the question of war and peace, and the path was clear to try the Soviet peace formula as government policy.

* Attempts have been made since 1917 to explain the Kerensky-Tereshchenko-Nekrasov combination, as well as some other features of Russian politics in this decade, by references to a bond of freemasonry. The theory is attractive in that it can be made to explain several phenomena: the rapid rise of Tereshchenko, the ties of the Kerensky group with more conservative ministers such as Konovalov, a link with the Soviet leadership via Chkheidze. However, the evidence is so scanty and contradictory that it defies any definite conclusions. This author is inclined to doubt that masonic ties had any great importance in the post-February politics (whatever role it may have played before 1917). There are other explanations for the alignments and politics of 1917, as well as evidence that the revolution broke whatever political unity the masonic organizations had. For a good survey of the problem, together with a new brief but useful piece of testimony from V. A. Obolensky, see N. Smith, "Russian Freemasonry."

PEACE THROUGH A SOCIALIST CONFERENCE

During the first coalition government Russian foreign policy reflected the composite nature of the government. Throughout May and June, Russia presented to the outside world not only two separate though related policies but also two separate agencies of implementation—the Soviet and the Foreign Ministry. On the one hand, there was the technically unofficial policy of the Soviet leaders: to organize an international socialist conference at Stockholm to discuss the conditions under which peace might be forced on the belligerents and to rally public opinion in the warring countries behind such a peace. The Stockholm movement was based primarily on socialist internationalism and only secondarily on an appreciation of Russian national needs, although the two seemed happily to coincide in this instance. On the other hand, there was the official or governmental phase of Russian foreign policy: to seek a revision of Allied war aims via traditional diplomatic channels and to promote an interallied conference for that purpose. This dual policy developed out of Soviet insistence that certain peace efforts could best be made through the socialist international, and others could best be carried out through government channels. Acceptance of this approach to international relations, which had been a prerequisite for Soviet participation in the government, was reflected in the new government program issued on May 5 that adopted the Soviet formula of "a peace without annexations or indemnities, and based on the rights of nations to decide their own affairs," and promised to try to persuade the Allies to adopt that formula.[1]

The two aspects of Russian foreign policy were closely intertwined, and the line between the Soviet and government spheres of activity was sometimes blurred. Coordination was to be ensured by the overlapping of personnel, especially in the person of Tsereteli, who maintained his ascendancy in the Executive Committee and established himself as the most authoritative member of the government. Kerensky, the only person who could challenge Tsereteli's position in the cabinet and who was its preeminent public figure, also accepted the Soviet peace program, as did the other key cabinet figures, Lvov, Tereshchenko, and Chernov. It was planned that the two policies would complement each other, but that the interallied conference would be delayed until the socialist conference had influenced public opinion in the Allied countries enough to force their governments to take real steps toward peace. Otherwise, according to the Soviet view, the imperialist governments would block any peace moves.[2] Tereshchenko, in a statement to the press on June 6, acknowledged the interplay of the interallied and international socialist conferences: government policies must consider the aspirations and desires of democratic elements, he said, and therefore the socialist conference, by clarifying such desires, would create a favorable ground for the government's policies.[3]

The Soviet leaders had already begun efforts to convene an international socialist conference at Stockholm. The idea for a socialist conference to work out a peace program, current in socialist circles ever since the outbreak of the war, was especially strong in the neutral countries and in Russia, but it had never gained much support among the socialists of other belligerent countries. All attempts to bring the socialists together had foundered on national animosity, especially on the part of the French and Belgian socialists, who refused to sit at the table with the German socialists as long as they supported their government in the war. Then came the Russian revolution and the apparent influence of the socialist parties in the new Russia, coinciding with the war-weariness that swept over Europe in the spring of 1917. This combination of factors seemed to offer fresh hope for uniting international socialism and bringing pressure on the belligerents to end the war.

Two attempts to convoke an international socialist conference were made in Western Europe immediately after and in response to the Russian revolution, the first by the Dutch and Scandinavian socialist parties. Working in part through the International Socialist Bureau of the Second International, they formed the Dutch-Scandinavian Committee, and on April 9/22 sent invitations to the various socialist parties to attend a conference to convene May 15/28 at Stockholm. The Allied socialist parties, except for their left-wing Minority, promptly refused to meet with the Germans.* The German socialists gave the conference their cautious support, which only increased the suspicion of both the Allied socialists and governments and led to the charge that the conference was German inspired. It was obvious to the Dutch-Scandinavian Committee that the only way the opposition of the Allied socialists could be overcome was to enlist the prestige and support of the socialist leaders of the Russian revolution. To this end the Danish Social Democratic leader Frederick Borgbjerg was sent to Petrograd.[4]

The second attempt was made by the International Socialist Committee, the executive organ created at the Zimmerwald and Kienthal conferences of antiwar socialists. This body issued a call on April 27 to all socialist groups adhering to the Zimmerwald position to meet just prior to the conference called by the Dutch-Scandinavian Committee. Since these groups were a minority in the socialist parties of Europe, the Third Zimmerwald Conference, as this was called, was considered by its proponents to be more a supplementary than a competing conference. The most radical of the Zimmerwaldists, however, considered the Stockholm Conference called by the Dutch-Scandinavian group a fraud perpetrated by the Majority socialists.[5]

Onto this scene, with two organizations already issuing calls

* The terms Minority and Majority represent political terminology of the war years that cannot be entirely avoided. When used with capitals, they refer to political positions, not numbers. The Majority refers to the socialists who supported the war effort of their countries, the Minority to those who took an antiwar position. The Majority tended in fact to be a numerical majority, but this was not invariably the case.

for an international socialist conference, moved the Petrograd Soviet. The appeal of March 14, calling for the unity of the workers of all countries to end the war, had been an implicit call for such a conference. However, it was only a statement of principles without concrete proposals concerning their implementation. On March 30, Liber suggested to the All-Russian Conference of Soviets that the Russian socialist parties take the initiative in calling an international socialist conference to work out the conditions for a general peace and to take measures to realize that peace.[6] No action was taken on his proposal, however; the resolution on the war passed by the Conference of Soviets again spoke only abstractly of the common effort of the peoples of all countries for peace. Finally, on April 11, the Executive Committee took more definite steps, instructing its Department of International Relations (which began to function April 1) to take the initiative in preparing for the convocation of an international socialist conference.[7]

The question of the conference was again put on the agenda of the Executive Committee when Borgbjerg arrived in Petrograd on April 14 to talk with the Soviet leaders. He brought two separate but related messages. One was an invitation to the Soviet and the Russian socialists to attend the conference called by the Dutch-Scandinavian Committee. The other was a message from the German Social Democratic Party stating that Germany was willing to negotiate a peace, and that no offensive would be undertaken by Germany against Russia. The invitation from the Dutch-Scandinavian Committee was favorably received by the Executive Committee, but not so the peace program of the German Social Democrats: the Soviet leaders thought it tantamount to an offer of a separate peace.[8] A decision on the invitation of the Dutch-Scandinavian Committee was postponed, however, until April 15, when the question of the conference was thoroughly discussed at an Executive Committee meeting. The discussion centered on the question of who should be invited to attend the conference. A small group led by the Bolsheviks argued that participation should be limited to the parties and factions that had opposed the war and the political truce in the warring countries, essentially the Minority socialists. Most of the Executive Committee, however, felt that all socialist groups had to be invited, insisting that it would be impossible to gain wide support for a peace program if the socialists who had supported their countries' war efforts, the bulk of the socialist parties of Europe, were excluded.[9]

At the same session the Executive Committee decided to take the initiative and issue their own invitation, on the grounds that both the Dutch-Scandinavian and the International Socialist Committee's proposals were too narrow and were therefore unacceptable to various groups. They believed that since the Soviet contained within itself a wide spectrum of socialist views, it was in the best position to appeal to all groups.[10] Moreover, they were very proud of the prestige that the revolution had given them among European socialists and were not inclined to take second place to the Dutch and the Scandinavians in reconvening the International, which they assumed they would dominate by virtue of their revolution. Their self-esteem was reinforced by the flood of letters and telegrams from every country that poured into the Executive Committee in April and May encouraging them to lead the way to peace. Ramsay MacDonald, leader of the antiwar minority of the British Labour Party (and future Prime Minister), wrote to this effect to Emile Vandervelde, a prominent Belgian socialist leader and cabinet minister, who passed the letter on to the Soviet leaders during a visit in May. In it MacDonald emphasized that the Soviet leaders must realize they had to act not simply in the interests of Russia but in the interests of the entire world democracy, and that they must formulate a peace program for the democracy of all of Europe.[11] The pride of the Soviet leaders did not escape Vandervelde, who observed after his visit that the Russian socialists thought the prestige of the revolution would enable them to impose their peace formula on the other socialist parties. Tsereteli believed, wrote Vandervelde, "that the services rendered to socialism by the Russian revolution gave him

some sort of right to pose as arbiter in an international conference."[12] This attitude reflected the anomalous chauvinism the
Soviet leaders developed, the notion that they had something—
a spirit, a wisdom, a message revealed by the revolution—that
the rest of Europe not only lacked but needed and that they
alone could provide. This sentiment, although rarely stated explicitly, is constantly present in Soviet speeches and writings,
and foreshadows in milder form the messianism of triumphant
Bolshevism.

On May 2, at the height of the government crisis, the Soviet
issued an appeal for an international socialist conference. Filled
with fiery rhetoric, it declared that the Russian revolution was
not just a national revolution but "the first stage in a world
revolution which will end the baseness of war and bring peace
to mankind." It called for a negotiated peace and for the socialists of all the warring countries to force their governments
to make peace on the basis of the Soviet formula. All socialist
factions were exhorted to join in the international conference
called by the Soviet to work toward this goal.[13] At the same time
the Soviet issued an appeal to the Russian army, designed to
counter any tendency of the soldiers to lay down arms in the
belief that peace was just around the corner.[14] Tsereteli, defending this appeal in the Soviet, emphasized one of the central
arguments of Revolutionary Defensism, which was to be stressed
more and more during the summer of 1917—that the peace program of the Soviet could be successful only if the Russian army
remained strong.

What sort of impression would it make on the people of the world if
our appeal to them was accompanied by a catastrophe at the front?
The governments of other countries would say to their people, point-
ing to us: they call you to follow their example, and this is what it leads
to. They would destroy you, as they destroy themselves.[15]

With the end of the government crisis on May 5, the Soviet
leaders were able to settle down to the difficult task of winning
the support of the Allied socialists for the conference. There
was no doubt that the Minority socialists would support the con-

ference. Nevertheless, the Soviets wished to talk with the leaders of the Minority groups about the conference and about concerted socialist action, for they were generally closer to the Soviet position than were the Majority socialists. On April 24 the Executive Committee's Department of International Relations had sent a telegram to the French Minority socialists, the British Socialist Party, the British Independent Labour Party, and the Italian Social Democratic Party, inviting them to send representatives to Petrograd. At the same time it relayed an appeal through the Foreign Ministry to the British, French, and Italian governments, asking them not to hinder the departure of these representatives for Petrograd. Nevertheless, those who tried were blocked in various ways and never got to Russia.[16]

The Allied Majority socialists represented another, more serious problem. Before the revolution the Allied parties had rejected the idea of a socialist conference during the war, and the French party had already rejected the invitation of the Dutch-Scandinavian Committee. Therefore, a special effort was needed to gain their acquiesence. The Executive Committee discussed the proposed conference with Marcel Cachin and Marius Moutet, two of the French Majority socialists who had come to Russia to convince the Soviet leaders to support the war effort. By the time of their departure on May 3, Cachin and Moutet had been won over by the Russians and promised to try to persuade their party not only to participate in the conference but to press the French government to revise its war aims along the lines of the Russian formula.[17] Albert Thomas, who remained in Petrograd and who had more influence with both the French Socialist Party and the French government, equivocated. He telegraphed French Prime Minister Ribot on May 2 that he was of the opinion that the French socialists should not curtly decline the invitation, but should insist that they could not attend unless the invitation was redrawn so as to exclude the German Majority socialists. However, in another telegram, received in France on May 9, he warned against an intransigent attitude.[18] A few days later he wrote to the British Prime Minister, Lloyd

George, that he felt it was necessary to go to the conference even without having first obtained the desired conditions, if the Russians were prepared to go without them. "If my Government concurs, I have decided to go to Stockholm at any cost. I sent word by telegram to my friends in France to accept participation in the Stockholm Conference."[19] Thomas soon changed his mind again, however, and decided against Stockholm, perhaps because the French government did not concur. Vacillation marked his actions throughout 1917.

The Soviet leaders met the strongest opposition from the Belgian socialists, whose delegation, led by Vandervelde, arrived in Petrograd on May 5. The purpose of the Belgian mission was threefold: to discourage peace sentiment in Russia, to plead the case of invaded Belgium before the Russians, and to discuss the Stockholm Conference.[20] The Belgians were the most intransigent of the Allied socialists on the matter of the conference, absolutely refusing to meet with the German Majority as long as they continued to support their government. Despite sharp disagreement on this point and others, the Soviet leaders, according to Tsereteli, established closer relations with Vandervelde's group than with any of the other socialist delegations because of the personal qualities of the Belgians, their sympathetic understanding of the feelings and conditions of the Russian workers and soldiers, and the widespread compassion felt for the plight of Belgium.[21] Still, the Belgians found their warmest reception in the extreme right of the Soviet. It is revealing that all the articles published by Vandervelde and his companion, Henri DeMan, appeared in Georgii V. Plekhanov's *Edinstvo* and in *Volia Naroda*, both on the right wing of the Russian socialist press.[22]

On May 20 another Allied socialist arrived to talk with the Soviet. This was Arthur Henderson, leader of the British Labour Party and member of the War Cabinet. The British, like the French, had rejected earlier calls for an international conference but felt the Russian call had to be considered more seriously. On May 8/21 the British Cabinet decided to send

Henderson to Russia in a capacity similar to Thomas's. At this meeting, Henderson expressed his own opposition to the Stockholm Conference, but thought that the British should attend if it took place. The attitude of the government at this time seems to have been favorable, and the minutes of the meeting indicate that the earlier British Labour delegation to Russia had been ordered to wait in Norway, in case its members were needed to attend the conference.[23] Originally a delegation headed by Henderson but representing all wings of British labor had been organized, in accordance with the Soviet request to meet members of the Minority. However, when the Seamen's Union refused to transport the antiwar leader Ramsay MacDonald, Henderson made the trip alone, joining Thomas and Vandervelde to form a troika of Allied socialist-ministers to negotiate with the Soviet leaders. Henderson's initial attitude was something of a shock to the Soviets. He informed Tsereteli that the Stockholm Conference was meeting strong opposition in England. When Tsereteli expressed surprise and stated that he understood the British government was favorably inclined, Henderson told him it was the British Labour Party, not the government, that was cool toward Stockholm: "In order to understand the difference between my attitude and Buchanan's [British ambassador], it is necessary to remember that if we decide to go to Stockholm then the pleasure of meeting with the Germans will be mine and not Buchanan's."[24] That the British government might be more favorable to Stockholm than the Labour Party was a novel and disconcerting notion. Fortunately for the Russians' peace of mind, the situation was soon reversed.

A series of meetings and conferences was held with the French, British, and Belgian leaders, who visited Petrograd, Moscow, and the front, but they brought little agreement. An incident in Moscow clearly revealed the distance separating the Russian and Allied socialists. When a spokesman for the Moscow Soviet expressed regret at the lukewarm reception the Russian peace program had received among the Allied socialists,

Thomas first stated that the Allies agreed with the Russian program, but then attached such a profusion of conditions to the Soviet formula as to effectively negate his own statement. In one sentence he revealed the gap more clearly than he probably realized: "But if Germany accepts our point of view [on returning Alsace-Lorraine to France and paying reparations for war damages], then we can participate in an international conference."[25] Such a condition effectively precluded any conference and was in direct conflict with both the Soviet formula and the Soviet goal of avoiding laying down any prior demands and conditions for participation. The wide disparity in the attitudes of the two sides was revealed in many other ways. For example, Henderson at one point suggested that the Russians look ahead to the discussion of the war by the British Trades Union Congress, scheduled for September, a suggestion that was greeted with chagrin: the Russians felt the war would be—and must be—ended by then.[26] On June 19 *Izvestiia* wrote, with a slight tone of desperation, that the European comrades did not understand the urgency of the situation: an international socialist conference could not be postponed one day! The two sides were thinking in fundamentally different terms about the imperativeness of the peace talks.

Meanwhile, the Executive Committee of the Petrograd Soviet continued with preparations for the conference, establishing a special commission on May 8 to work on the project.[27] The commission included some of the most important members of the Soviet leadership: Tsereteli, Chkheidze, Gots, Dan, and Rozanov. At a meeting on May 15, the commission, following the line of the Executive Committee discussions on April 25, reaffirmed that the Executive Committee should take the exclusive initiative for convening the conference and for its organization. To avoid misunderstandings, communications should be sent to the Dutch-Scandinavian and International Socialist committees explaining the tactical considerations leading to this decision and making clear that the assistance of these groups would be welcomed. The commission also agreed on Stockholm as the meeting place and June 18/July 1 as the opening date, and that all recognized socialist and workers' groups willing to undertake a general struggle to force the belligerents to accept the Soviet peace formula would be invited. The details of how to wage such a struggle would be left to the conference. The commission met again on May 17, primarily to work out the composition of the Russian delegation, and decided to give the Soviet effective control of it.[28]

On May 18 the commission reported to the Executive Committee and presented a draft of a statement to be sent to all socialist parties and trade unions about the Stockholm conference.[29] News reached Petrograd the same day that on May 15 a French Socialist Party conference, influenced by Cachin and Moutet, had voted to attend the conference. This news undoubtedly encouraged the Soviet leaders to push ahead. On the 20th the commission's statement was approved and published. For the first time, the specific steps to be taken in convoking the conference were spelled out.

The first necessary and decisive step in the organization of such an international movement [a union of the world democracy in favor of peace] is the convocation of an international conference. Its main task must be an agreement among the representatives of the socialist proletariat in regard to the liquidation of the policy of "national unity" with the imperialistic governments and classes which excludes the possibility of a struggle for peace and of finding ways and means for carrying out this struggle. . . .

All parties and organizations of the toiling classes which share these views and are prepared to unite their efforts in order to carry them into effect are invited by the Soviet to take part in the proposed conference.

The Soviet expresses in connection with this its firm conviction that all the parties and organizations which accept this invitation will take upon themselves the obligation to carry out unfailingly all the decisions which the conference adopts.

The Soviet chooses Stockholm as the place for the conference. The time for the conference is June 28–July 8, 1917.[30]

The issuance of the invitation of May 20, following on the vote of the French Socialist Party and at least partial acceptance of the conference by the other Allied socialist delegations, marked the high tide of success for the Stockholm venture. The first of a series of reverses that were to deal a mortal blow to the conference followed quickly on the heels of the invitation. News soon reached Petrograd that the French government had announced on May 19/June 1 it would not issue passports to French socialists to attend the conference.[31] This announcement was followed by a stormy four-day secret session of the Chamber of Deputies, ending in a vote of confidence for the government and a confirmation of its decision.[32] The Italian government soon followed suit; Italian socialists would not be given passports. The United States had already refused to issue passports on May 9/22, but this move was more a psychological blow to the conference than a genuine setback, since the American socialists were small in numbers and influence. The British government alone still watched and waited, and on this the Soviets pinned great hope.

Meanwhile, difficulties developed between the Soviet leaders and the Allied socialists who were in Petrograd. Although the visiting delegates had given general approval to the conference and to the Soviet's peace formula, all attempts to work out a specific program for the conference proved futile, primarily because the Allies desired certain preconditions and guarantees on points the Soviets preferred to leave open. The dispute, which dragged on through May and June, centered on three issues. The first was whether the question of responsibility for the war and the disruption of the International should be raised at the conference. The Allied socialists, especially the French, insisted that the first item on the agenda at Stockholm should be the question of Germany's guilt and the role of the German socialists in supporting the German war effort. The Soviets opposed this on the grounds that such a condition would wreck the conference before it started. In addition, the Soviet leaders contended that the war was caused by the imperialistic rivalry of all the capitalist governments. The second issue concerned the political situation inside the warring countries. The Allied socialists insisted that the German Majority socialists renounce the *Burgfrieden*, their political truce with the German government and the bourgeois parties, before the conference, but the Soviets objected that it would be unfair to force the Germans to make such a move without a similar requirement of the Allies. Moreover, they believed a repudiation of the political truce should come after the conference had convened, as a simultaneous action by all socialist parties in all countries. Finally, at issue was the question of whether the decisions of the conference were to be binding on all participants, as the Soviet leaders desired. The Allied socialists flatly refused to participate under such a condition.[33]

The Soviet's May 20 invitation to a conference brought these issues into sharper focus. Earlier statements had been conveniently vague, but this one was specific, naming a date, a place, and the conditions for a meeting. Thomas, Vandervelde, and Henderson, who had been touring Russia when the Executive Committee voted its approval, were greatly upset upon hearing of the action and immediately expressed their objections. They arranged a meeting with Tsereteli, Skobelev, and Kerensky to discuss the Soviet move and the sharpening disagreements between the two sides.* The three Allied socialists demanded to know why the Russians had chosen to play an independent role, both in initiating the Stockholm Conference and in raising objections to an Allied socialist conference,† instead of acting jointly with them, as one of the Allies. Tsereteli replied that the Soviet had to act independently, since it wished to serve as a conciliating force between the two enemy blocs. Although the Soviet leaders finally agreed to send an observer to an Allied socialist conference in London,[34] the meeting was not especially

---

* Though the date of the meeting is not certain, it probably took place on May 21. Vandervelde's itinerary lists a meeting with Tsereteli and Skobelev on that date, but shows no other meeting with members of the Soviet between May 20 and May 23, when he departed for the front.

† In early May the British Labour Party had invited the Executive Party to join in an interallied socialist conference in London, an invitation that was repeated by Henderson when he arrived in Petrograd. The Executive Committee refused. Pokrovskii and Iakovlev, I (*Protokoly*), 221: session of bureau of May 6; Vandervelde, "Rapport," p. 34.

successful, and the main points of dissension remained un-resolved. The three Allies drew up a formal letter of protest against the Soviet's action, repeating their demands for certain preconditions and guarantees about the agenda.[35] In a reply on May 30, the Executive Committee argued that acceptance of the Soviet peace formula was a sufficient basis of agreement for attending the conference; there was no need for detailed preliminary agreements and agendas, nor was it necessary to lay down certain conditions for participation. "This could cre-ate the appearance of irreconcilable contradictions where, dur-ing a general discussion, the spirit of proletarian solidarity would be instrumental in seeking out a decision that would be equally acceptable to all."[36] The Soviet leaders were optimistic-ally hoping that the conference would generate its own spirit of brotherhood and conciliation, a spirit that would overcome some of the seemingly insurmountable hostilities and differ-ences. In this, they showed either great faith in international socialism or great naïveté.

Even as the Soviet leaders were meeting increased opposition from the Allies, their Petrograd base was eroding away, a pro-cess that alarmed them but did not command their full atten-tion. The volatile followers of the Soviet leaders expected a miraculous solution to their problems from the coalition gov-ernment, a utopian expectation that was clear in the remarks of a soldier delegate to the Petrograd Soviet: "Comrade Tsereteli has been Minister for ten whole days. What has been done for peace?"[37] It is possible that he was taking his cue from the Bol-sheviks, who encouraged this approach. Lenin wrote in *Pravda* on May 11 (less than a week after the government had taken office): "The coalition cabinet has brought no changes. The tsar's secret treaties remain sacred to it."[38] At times, the wide-spread belief in the leaders' ability to work miracles—and the dissatisfaction when they could not—expressed itself over triv-ial, even silly, matters. Witness the report of a Menshevik of-ficial of the Kazan Soviet of Workers' and Soldiers' Deputies, who was approached by a not uneducated woman with a request that the Soviet make her husband, who was living with another woman, come home. Upon being told that this was impossible, she replied: "What kind of authority are you if you cannot do even this?"[39]

The increasing discontent over the actions and inaction of the Soviet (which is probably a more accurate way of describing the negative sentiment growing among the workers and soldiers than to term it a rise in Bolshevik influence, as even Trotsky grudgingly acknowledged)[40] manifested itself in several ways. One reflection of the popular feeling can be seen in the votes in the district (raion) soviets in Petrograd: in May control of four of them passed into the hands of Bolsheviks or Bolshevik-led coalitions hostile to the Revolutionary Defensist leadership of the Petrograd Soviet.[41] This period also saw the beginning of the recall of delegates to the Petrograd Soviet by factories and garrisons, and their replacement by more radical deputies, a process that by September would give the Bolsheviks a majority.

Also indicative was the split in Menshevik ranks between the Petrograd Mensheviks and the All-Russian Conference held May 7–11. The conference, firmly controlled by the same Revolutionary Defensists who dominated the Petrograd Soviet, voted approval of the Soviet leaders' tactics and policies. Immediately thereafter, however, the Petrograd party organization passed into the hands of the left wing of the party, a group that increasingly assumed a distinct identity as the Menshevik-Internationalists and opposed both the coalition and the cautiousness of the Revolutionary Defensists in pursuing peace. Led by Martov, the Menshevik-Internationalists kept up a steady attack on Tsereteli and the official leadership during 1917. However, since they did not have a clear alternative to Tsereteli's peace program, they were largely reduced to simply criticizing his lack of success and stress on Defensism. Martov's call for an ultimatum to the Allies, to be followed by a "separate war" (he too drew back from a separate peace), aroused the enthusiasm of virtually nobody, though this quixotic idea was to find recurring expression among leftists desperately searching for an alternative to Tsereteli's Revolutionary Defensism on the one hand and Lenin's defeatism or a separate peace on the other. The Menshevik-Internationalists found a more specific point on which to base their attack against the leadership of Tsereteli and Dan after July, when they joined the clamor for an all-socialist or "all-democratic" government. By autumn they had succeeded in eroding the party base of the Revolutionary Defensists, but they were themselves unable to build a mass following as the Revolutionary Defensists had in the first months of 1917 and as the Bolsheviks would later. As they were taunted on more than one occasion, why should dissatisfied workers and soldiers settle for "Bolsheviks of the second sort" when they could have the genuine thing?[42]

An even more ominous sign of the precarious position of the Revolutionary Defensists came in June on the eve of the Russian offensive. The strength of antiwar sentiment and restiveness over lack of results was clearly revealed at a huge demonstration on June 18, which was sponsored by the All-Russian Congress of Soviets. Ostensibly organized to conciliate the Bolsheviks, whose own demonstration, planned for June 10, had been banned by the congress, the rally was intended to channel discontent into a show of support for the Soviet peace program and, by extension, for the Provisional Government. The plan misfired, however, and Bolshevik and anarchist slogans calling for peace and "all power to the Soviets" predominated.[43]

Numerous attempts were made by the Soviet Majority to popularize their position. They not only wrote editorials in their papers and used the soviets as their forums but also published hundreds of pamphlets during 1917 to educate and instruct the masses. The didactic nature and simple language of these pamphlets make their intent clear. One by Rozanov is typical. In it he presented both an explanation of the causes of the war (imperialist greed and secret diplomacy) and a solution (popular control of foreign relations, including the question of peace). The Russian peace efforts were having great impact abroad, he claimed (this is May), but time and patience were

needed for those efforts to be successful.[44] Though the explanation of the causes of the war probably had some appeal for the
pamphlet's readers, it is doubtful that they found Rozanov's
plea for patience attractive. Another pamphlet, better written
than most but still designed for popular consumption and typical, was produced by Voitinskii to explain the policies of the
coalition government. It emphasized the dangers of precipitate
action, which might lead to a rupture with the Allies, and the
need to preserve the army for the defense of the country and
the revolution against German imperialism.[45] Still another attempted to explain, in the simplest terms, how the Soviet program could lead to peace: "If the German people knew that we
do not desire to rob them or take revenge on them, then perhaps a way can be found to enter into peace negotiations." At
the same time, the writer warned that a separate peace would
lead to disaster, bringing down upon Russia either German imperialism or Allied vengeance.[46] The prospect of Allied vengeance was hardly likely to build trust in the Allies or strengthen
the alliance; furthermore, somehow the dangers of a separate
peace the author painted did not really sound worse than continued war. This was one of the major problems facing the
Soviet propagandists. They were forced into the position of
arguing that the satisfaction of immediate demands had to be
postponed for the sake of more important, long-range programs,
programs that did not in fact seem much more desirable, if at
all. There is virtually no way to tell how influential these tracts
were.

The Soviet leaders also made some effort to counter the Bolsheviks by sending members of the Soviet Majority to factory
and barrack meetings (where the Bolsheviks, excluded from top
Soviet circles, centered their activities). However, the effort was
half-hearted and not successful. The Soviet leaders did not fully
realize the importance of these meetings, and were too tied
down by the responsibilities of Soviet and government work
to give them much attention. The daily press of business and
their focus on broader national and international questions cut

them off from concern with the day-to-day issues at the local level. The Bolsheviks capitalized on this apparent lack of concern, suggesting at these meetings that the socialist ministers be invited to attend the next meeting to explain their policies. If the Soviet leaders did not appear (and obviously they could not attend hundreds of factory and garrison meetings, even had they wanted to), a resolution hostile to the government or the Soviet majority might then be passed by the disgruntled soldiers or workers.[47]

Despite the increasing signs of restiveness in Petrograd, the country as a whole still seemed securely behind the Revolutionary Defensists, as reflected in the composition of the All-Russian Congress of Soviets of Workers' and Soldiers' Deputies, which opened on June 3. The Tsereteli leadership found itself with a comfortable four or five to one majority. The Stockholm Conference and foreign policy held the center of the stage at the congress, which met at a time when there were still high hopes for the success of the Stockholm venture. The triumph of the French socialist vote had been offset by the decision of the French government not to issue passports, but that decision might still be reversed. The British government had not yet taken a position, but seemed favorably inclined. Negotiations with the Allied socialists had been exasperating, but agreement in principle existed, and there was some reason to believe that they would bend to the Soviet position as popular feeling in favor of peace grew in their countries. There were dark shadows cast by certain bellicose statements of various Allied leaders, but prospects still looked bright. How could they look otherwise? After the triumph over Tsarism and then over Miliukov, anything seemed possible. An exuberant mood still lingered on in Petrograd, despite the many and growing problems.

The dominant presidium group led by Tsereteli used the congress as a sounding board for its programs. In a report on war and peace, presented on behalf of the Executive Committee, Dan emphasized that peace must be concluded as soon as possible: the revolution must put an end to the war, before the

KERENSKY

MILIUKOV

CHERNOV

LIBER

CHKHEIDZE

AVKSENTEV

TSERETELI

PESHEKHONOV

GUCHKOV

RODZIANKO

V. D. Nabokov

Nekrasov

TSERETELI

war destroyed the revolution. He examined the two proposals that had been suggested as alternatives to the peace policy of the Executive Committee—the idea of a separate peace and the idea of a separate war—and rejected both as unrealistic and as courting disaster and ruin for Russia. The goal of the Russian democracy must continue to be a general peace based on the Soviet formula. To this end, said Dan, two steps were being taken: an attempt to organize an international socialist conference was under way, and the Provisional Government was seeking to persuade the Allied governments to accept the formula of "no annexations." Meanwhile, the effectiveness of both the Soviet and the government programs depended on the Russian army remaining strong and active, so as to give weight to Russia's voice.[48] In conclusion, Dan introduced a resolution that branded the war an attempt of imperialists to get new markets and bring weak states under their economic and political control. The resolution rejected both a separate peace and a war to total victory on the grounds that either course would intensify the conditions that made the war possible rather than eliminate them. Thus, the present program was the correct one:

In view of the fact that war can be brought to an end only through the united efforts of the democracies of all countries, the Congress regards as essential (a) that the Russian revolutionary democracy, through its organ, the All-Russian Soviet, should address itself to the democracies of all States, asking them to join in the rallying cry: "Peace without annexation and indemnity, and on the basis of self-determination of peoples"—and try to influence their governments along these lines; (b) that it (Russian democracy) should make every effort to reestablish the international labor solidarity, to work out definite peace terms, and means to put them into force.[49]

The resolution, which passed readily, also protested the Allies' denial of passports for the conference and urged the Provisional Government to continue its efforts to persuade the Allies to reexamine their treaties, with a view to abandoning a policy of conquest. Meanwhile, it concluded, until such time as peace could be attained, the army must be ready for military action, both defensive and offensive.

With the advantage of hindsight, it can be seen that, to some extent, the emphasis on military preparedness as a major factor in Russian foreign policy at this congress represented the beginning of a drift away from the sanguine hopes about the Stockholm Conference. The Soviet leaders were coming to realize that it would not be as easy to organize the conference as they had thought. However, they still believed it was possible; indeed, their entire policy was based on the premise that such a conference could be arranged.

Faced with the ominous signs of growing foreign and domestic opposition, the Soviet leaders launched two undertakings in an effort to bolster their foreign policy and the Stockholm Conference. One move was in the right direction, but it was not vigorously pushed; the other flew in the face of popular opinion and was a disastrous mistake. First, the Soviet leaders tried to whip up popular support abroad for Stockholm, in the hope that this would bring new pressure on the Allied governments to grant passports and turn toward peace on the Soviet formula. The All-Russian Congress of Soviets voted to send a delegation abroad to advance the cause of the conference through both organizational work and publicity, and after several delays a delegation of four Social Democrats and one Socialist Revolutionary, all adherents of the Soviet Majority, arrived in Stockholm on June 22. A week later they merged with the Dutch-Scandinavian group to pool their efforts and resources on behalf of the Stockholm Conference. Some of the Russian delegates then proceeded to the Allied countries to try to gain support for the conference, while the others remained in Stockholm to establish a headquarters.[50]

As these activities were launched in Western Europe, the Soviet leaders took the second—and disastrous—step: they lent their support to a plan for a Russian military offensive, an undertaking they hoped would aid their cause by impressing both the Allied and the enemy governments of Russia's continuing status as a great power. The leading spirit of this venture, which gained the reluctant support of the Petrograd Soviet and most of the socialist press, was Minister of War Kerensky, who still had nominal ties with the Soviet. In part, the acquiescence of the Soviet leaders seems to have been the price they had to pay for the support of the other members of the coalition government for their peace program. More important, however, they apparently believed the plan would bolster that program. The Soviet arguments for strengthening the army and for the offensive centered on two points: 1) Russia must be prepared to undertake active military operations as a means of defending the gains of the revolution, for if she remained inactive and thereby enabled Germany to defeat the Western Allies, Germany would then turn on Russia and destroy the revolution; and 2) the Russian army must be restored to its full combat potential, so that Russia could negotiate with her Allies and enemies from a position of strength.

At first the socialist advocates of the offensive proceeded cautiously. In a May 14 editorial, *Delo Naroda* declared there was no need for the "panicky fear and superstitious terror" that the word offensive created in some democratic circles. Three days later *Izvestiia* asserted that "the immediate question is not an offensive, but creating *the possibility of an offensive*" (italics in the original). This possibility would enable Russia's representatives to speak with more authority internationally and would prevent the Germans from transferring enough troops to the Western front to crush the French and the British.[51] Still, the popular mood was such that when an antiwar paper, *Novaia Zhizn*, charged the government with concentrating entirely on the preparations for an offensive and ignoring peace efforts, *Izvestiia* found it necessary to answer on the same day, insisting the charge was not true: the many appeals for improving the army did not mean any change in the peace policy of the Soviet and the government.[52]

By the time the All-Russian Congress of Soviets was convened, the initial caution on the subject of the offensive was beginning to fade. Tsereteli spoke out more boldly on the question, arguing that the army must not only be strengthened but even be readied for an offensive, in order to prepare the way for the successful negotiation of a universal peace.[53] The congress's resolution on the war stated that until the war was brought to an end by the "united efforts of the democracies of all countries," the Russian army had to be prepared for either offensive or defensive action. The resolution had hedged, however, by insisting that the decision on whether or not to take the offensive ought to be based exclusively on military and strategic considerations.

The moderate socialists who favored an offensive made wide use of this equivocation, finding in it a way to advance the idea of an offensive without openly advocating it, and even a way to rationalize this unpalatable step to themselves. To blunt the effects of this distasteful task and lessen the risk of losing support, they approached the subject indirectly. Limiting themselves to talk of "preparedness for an offensive" and "ability to undertake offensive operations," they dodged the main issue of whether an offensive would or should be undertaken by deferring at that point to "strategic considerations." The delicacy of the question in Soviet circles is well illustrated in Voitinskii's pamphlet, in which he took great pains to point out that the defensive or aggressive character of a war is determined by its aims, not by its military strategy, and that a purely defensive war may require offensive operations.[54] This problem of definition, which obviously troubled the Soviet leaders, was made the more difficult by the fact that the adjective *nastypatelnyi* was used for both "offensive" operations and "aggressive" war aims, and the two ideas were evidently linked in the popular mind.

For the Soviet leaders, the decision to support the offensive, together with the emphasis on strengthening the army embodied in the second point of the coalition government's program, was a drastic error that warped their entire policy. Voitinskii, in looking back at the relationship between the Soviet leaders' support of the army and their foreign policy, went straight to the heart of the problem: the Soviet leaders confused the means and the end. In the ideology of Revolutionary Defensism, the maintenance of the army had been perceived only as a means of defending Russia until peace could be worked out. However, as the peace offensive bogged down, more attention was given to the army and to a military advance as a way to salvage the peace policy, thus placing an emphasis on the army— the means—far out of proportion to its original role, and less energy was devoted directly to the end—the faltering Stockholm Conference. Despite Voitinskii's perception, he shows the same blind spots that led the Soviet leaders into the impasse, for though he saw their mistake, he held to the line of reasoning that had trapped them: "an 'energetic' foreign policy led to a rupture with the allies and a separate peace," and an energetic domestic policy led to a rupture of the coalition and a Soviet dictatorship. "We wished to avoid both," he wrote, "but did not see a way to resolve these two problems, and this led to that fatal procrastination which so characterized this period of the revolution."[55]

No matter how the presidium group explained the relationship between their peace offensive and a military offensive, it was obvious to all that they were supporting the military offensive, and in so doing, were cutting the ground from beneath their own feet. The argument that, ultimately, peace would be brought nearer by an offensive carried little weight at a time when antiwar sentiment was very strong, especially in Petrograd. The idea of an offensive was simply repugnant to the soldiers and workers. Given this attitude and the state of the army, it was a tremendous gamble for the Soviet leaders to stake their foreign policy, indeed their entire future, on the offensive. That they did so indicates more than a confusion of means and ends; it indicates the extent to which their peace offensive was faltering, and their great concern over the Allies' indifference to Russian demands for peace moves. Difficulties encountered by the government in carrying out its part of the peace effort— to persuade the Allies to revise their war aims—help explain the Soviet support for an offensive. We turn, then, to the government's efforts to implement the new foreign policy.

PEACE THROUGH A REVISION OF WAR AIMS

While the Soviet was attempting to convoke the Stockholm Conference, the government made an effort to persuade the Allies to review and revise their stated war aims in order to remove all doubt about their imperialistic or aggressive intentions. The socialist and non-socialist members of the government alike considered this effort important, both because it improved the prospects for peace by showing the enemy that negotiations were possible and because it would revive the flagging morale of the army. The socialists continued to stress that the only way to prevent the disintegration of the army was to assure the soldiers the war was being continued for democratic and defensive purposes alone. As the belief spread among the troops that the war was being prolonged by French and British ambitions, the need to get the Allies to announce their adherence to the Soviet no-annexations formula became even more pressing. Hopefully, such a diplomatic triumph would convince the country that real progress was being made toward peace, halt the erosion of support for the Soviet majority, and give the government time to deal with its many serious problems. Revision of war aims thus came to be viewed as a kind of panacea for all problems, foreign and domestic, especially since both the Soviet and the government leaders felt—and probably rightly so—that little progress could be made on the domestic front as long as the war disrupted all normal activity.

The impetus for a general revision of Allied war aims came from Soviet circles, which demanded such a revision in almost all their resolutions on foreign policy and the war, as well as in countless editorials in the socialist press. However, though the new foreign policy formula had originated with the Soviet and the socialist ministers, its application was in the hands of For-

eign Ministry officials, who were concerned primarily with pro-
tecting Russian national interests. For a time in May and June
there seemed to be a unity of objectives between these national
interests and the Soviet program. The maintenance of this unity
and in fact the success of the foreign policy programs of both the
Provisional Government and the Soviet depended in large part
on the actions of the new Foreign Minister, Tereshchenko.

Even more than Kerensky and Tsereteli, Tereshchenko was
of that group of men who rose rapidly from obscurity to positions of great power and influence during the revolution. His
appointment as Minister of Finance in March had occasioned
considerable surprise. The newspapers had little more information than that he was very young (twenty-nine), a multimillion-
aire (through his interests in Ukrainian sugar beets), and a con-
noisseur of the theater and the ballet. Exactly how he rose to
prominence is not clear. Apparently he met a number of leading Duma figures through his work in the Russian Red Cross
and as head of the Kiev branch of the War Industries Committees, and from these contacts was drawn into the circle around
Nekrasov and Guchkov, a group that was plotting a palace revolution against Nicholas II. Beyond an acquaintance with European countries and languages, he had little training for the
office of Foreign Minister. He had, however, shown a keen interest in foreign affairs in the months after the revolution, and
in early April Miliukov had considered resigning in his favor.[1]
Moreover, as previously noted, he had the backing of Kerensky
for the post and was acceptable to both the Soviet leaders and
the non-socialists. A liberal who did not belong to any political
party, he joined Kerensky and Nekrasov in a triumvirate that
formed the core of the opposition to Miliukov and Guchkov in
the first cabinet and then dominated the cabinets after July.
Apart from Kerensky, he was the only man to hold a cabinet
post throughout the entire period of the Provisional Government. He seems to have been firmly attached to Kerensky, serv-
ing as his trusted lieutenant and associate throughout the entire
Provisional Government period. Not until the last month be-

fore the Bolshevik takeover did his optimism and his faith in Kerensky's leadership fail.

Evidence about Tereshchenko's views on foreign policy, much less his inner thoughts, is extremely scanty. He does not seem to have confided in associates, as Miliukov did, nor did he write current or retrospective works on his policies, as did both Miliukov and Tsereteli. Evaluations must therefore be based almost exclusively on his public actions in 1917. Unlike Tsereteli and Miliukov, Tereshchenko seems not to have had a long-range, clearly defined, ideologically supported view of foreign policy. He also lacked their drive and personal dynamism, sometimes appearing more a dilletante and an associate than a leader. There is a temptation to call him an opportunist or unprincipled, but the description does not quite fit. Rather, he seems to have been a pragmatic patriot who tried to steer through the constantly shifting shoals of revolutionary politics to bring Russia out of the war intact, with her traditional status preserved and her long-range interests guarded. To this end, he was willing to use any means at his disposal, not hesitating to change course.

How well-defined Tereshchenko's ideas about the immediate tasks of Russian foreign policy were at the time he took office is not entirely clear. He was an ardent nationalist, but he supported the policy of seeking peace and Allied acceptance of the Soviet formula of no annexations, in the belief that only in this way could the army be induced to continue fighting. He accepted the view that once the pacific and just objectives of Russia and her Allies had been clearly demonstrated to the army and the people, they would be willing to defend Russia if her enemies refused to accept her formula for a just peace. At the same time, he doubted that Germany would accept the negotiated peace envisioned by the Soviets until it became clear to her that she could neither win nor continue the war. He therefore considered the Soviet peace program valuable in that it would expose Germany's unwillingness to make peace and convince the Russian soldiers of the need to continue defending the country. On the crucial question of Constantinople and the Straits, he believed that Russia's interests would best be served by some form of neutralization.[2]

With this rather utilitarian view of the Soviet peace slogans, it might well be questioned whether Tereshchenko really accepted the Soviet program. One wonders if he merely took the position Kerensky had urged on Miliukov earlier: modify the language if not the content of Russian foreign policy! It appears that he followed both courses. He was realistic enough to learn from Miliukov's experience that he had to adopt the Soviet position on foreign policy, at least outwardly. In this connection, it should be pointed out that despite all talk of war aims revision, he carefully avoided throughout his tenure of office ever explicitly stating that Russia renounced control of the Straits, as promised by the Allies. At the same time he seems to have appreciated Russia's need for peace and to have genuinely desired an honorable settlement that would preserve Russia's frontiers and provide a resolution of the Straits and Balkans problems consistent with long-term Russian national interests. Being ambitious, and a bit vain, he must have been attracted by the thought of the diplomatic laurels that would come from presiding over an Allied conference to revise war aims (he wanted it to meet in Petrograd), not to mention the historical reputation and glory that would accrue to the man who successfully extracted Russia from the war, and he was willing to make use of the Soviet peace formula and the Stockholm Conference to that end.

The difficulty of implementing the new foreign policy line was made clear to Tereshchenko immediately. The Allied responses to the note of April 18 (the official transmittal of the declaration of March 27) were awaiting him when he took up his duties. Since the Allies had prepared their responses to the Russian note before Miliukov was toppled, it is not surprising that Tereshchenko found them objectionable. He immediately entered into negotiations with the Allied ambassadors, seeking a modification of the notes that would bring them more into line with the new outlook of Russian foreign policy and make them acceptable to the Soviet. The government's declaration of May 5, including its pronouncements on foreign policy, evidently was not officially communicated to the Allied governments. Nevertheless, the contents were known abroad, and a request from Kerensky to review the wartime treaties had been informally communicated; therefore, the government's new position had to be taken into consideration in revising the notes for publication.[3] Buchanan wrote to his Foreign Office on May 9/21, stating that publication of the British reply in its original form would cause trouble in Russia. "After discussing the question with Albert Thomas," he wrote, "I think that we ought to forestall any action of this kind by ourselves making some conciliatory but non-committal statement on the subject."[4]

The negotiations to revise the notes proceeded with some difficulty, but the Allies were willing to accede to some of Tereshchenko's suggestions. Tereshchenko was extremely worried about any word or phrase being interpreted in such a way as to imply that the Allies rejected the no-annexation formula or were adamant about total victory to the exclusion of a negotiated peace. A statement open to such interpretation would antagonize the Soviet and, he feared, undermine Kerensky's efforts to restore the army. The British and French notes were altered at the request of Tereshchenko (in the case of the British note three times) before he felt that they could safely be released.[5] Even as revised they hardly represented an acceptance of the Russian program, although a few concessions had been wrung from the Allies, and some of the more offensive sections had been deleted. Indeed, the unsatisfactory progress in this area was one factor that led the Soviet leaders to push ahead with the effort to convene the Stockholm Conference. After an unsuccessful meeting with Buchanan on May 26, they were more than ever convinced of the correctness of their view: only a successful appeal to the workers and socialists of the Allied countries would force the governments to revise their war aims and seek a negotiated peace.[6] The French note is especially interesting to examine, since the text of the original is available for comparison. Even as finally published, the French note was far from the Russian program. It referred to a "fight until victory," "reparatory indemnities," "indispensable guarantees," and of course the return of Alsace-Lorraine. Nevertheless, it was toned down from the original draft, which spoke of chastising the initiators of the war and of "the restitutions, reparations and guarantees required." A paragaraph referring to the improvement of the conditions "under which the Russian people propose to carry to victory the war against their adversaries" was dropped altogether. In a new paragraph in the final version, the French did pay lip service to the new Russian program, which, however feeble, was more than the Italians were prepared to do in their note.[7] Only the British note made any real concession to the Russian program and directly mentioned a general revision of agreements. After making the same sort of general statement found in all the replies (Britain fought only for the triumph of law, right, justice, and had no designs for conquest or domination over other peoples), the British note concluded: "but if the Russian Government so desires they [the British] are quite ready with their Allies to examine, and, if need be, to revise these agreements."[8] This sentence evidently was included during the revision of the note. What the Russians did not know was that during these negotiations the War Cabinet had become concerned, so concerned that they established a committee headed by Prime Minister Lloyd George to review policy as a whole and report on "the Naval, Military, and Political situations."[9]

The American response to the April 18 note was especially important to the Russians. They were hopeful that the United States would support their position, given the past statements of President Wilson. The no annexations or indemnities, self-determination of peoples slogan was in a sense his as well as the Soviet's. There was, however, a difference in both the purpose and the use of the slogan. The Soviet viewed it as the basis of an *immediate, negotiated* peace; Wilson saw it as the basis of a *future* peace *imposed by victory*. Therefore, Tereshchenko was not only disappointed by Wilson's message; he was singularly unsuccessful in getting any revisions made in it.[10] There was an important fact that Tereshchenko and the Soviet leaders did not know: after the United States entered the war, Wilson had decided that nothing more should be done about peace terms, and that all such statements should wait until the war had been won.[11] The British, however, had been informed of the American position by Wilson's intimate advisor, Colonel House.[12] They could thus afford to appear willing to talk about peace terms, knowing full well that the United States would oppose the talks.

The rather vague acceptance by the British of the proposal for a review and a revision of the treaty arrangements, and the even more vague French statement, were negated by the general rebuff of the Russian formula the notes contained. The entire exchange indicated the distance that separated Russian and Allied thinking. Quite apart from the question of a willingness or unwillingness to give up annexations and indemnities, the two sides viewed the matter of war aims revision from fundamentally different perspectives. The Russian government had accepted the Revolutionary Defensist credo that a public revision of war aims would bolster the will of the Russian soldier to fight. The Allies believed that, on the contrary, talk of war aims and imminent peace negotiations undermined the will to fight, not only in the Russian army but in their own armies as well. Accordingly, all such discussion should be postponed as long as possible, so as not to adversely affect the war effort. The British War Cabinet officially so decided on July 3/16.[13] Procrastination, but not outright refusal to discuss war aims, was judged, correctly, to be the best way to humor the Russians without giving up anything.

The response of the Allies caused Tereshchenko to hesitate. He was inclined to seize on the vague acceptance, ignore the rebuff, and push ahead by laying down in more specific terms the future peace that Russia envisioned. He consulted Tsereteli, but the latter demurred. He believed the Russian government should refrain from the "concretization" of peace terms until the international socialist conference had gained wider support for the Soviet peace formula in the Allied countries. Tereshchenko agreed.[14] On May 24 he sent a telegram to the Russian chargé d'affaires in London, and presumably similar ones to other Russian representatives abroad, stating "We consider that at the present moment it would not be in our interest to call for an immediate exchange of views with the Allies on this matter." That moment would come, he said, when the situation at the front had been improved and unanimity with regard to the final aims of the war had been reached with the British representatives, Buchanan and Henderson, in Petrograd.[15]

Tereshchenko's plan to postpone the calling of an interallied conference until a more propitious moment was upset by the reaction within Russia to the publication of the Allied notes. All his efforts to revise the notes were not enough to prevent an outcry in the socialist press, although he possibly blunted it. The pro-Soviet papers were outraged by the empty phrases of the Allied notes and the United States message. *Rabochaia Gazeta* charged bluntly that "the English and French bourgeoisie are prepared to change their flag, but under the new flag they desire to carry the old cargo."[16] *Izvestiia* stated that the British and French notes would not find much enthusiasm among the Russian people. "Russian democracy does not see the embodiment of this principle [peace without open or veiled annexations and indemnities] in the notes from France and England. On the contrary. Alongside the recognition of the 'principles' it sees a tendency to subsume under this principle the old aims that are contradictory to it."[17] Of Wilson's message, *Izvestiia* wrote:

There is no need to speak very much about this message. President Wilson is mistaken if he thinks that such thoughts can find acceptance in the hearts of the revolutionary people of Russia. The Russian revolutionary democracy knows only too well that the path to universal peace—so fervently awaited—lies only in a united struggle of all the workers in the world against world imperialism."[18]

Despite their angry charges, the Soviet papers made a desperate attempt to find some acceptance of the Russian program in the Allied notes. *Izvestiia* seized on the British consent to examine and perhaps revise the treaties as "the consent of the Allied powers to *a revision of agreements* in accordance with the principles proclaimed by our Provisional Government" (italics in original).[19] Moreover, it added, the revolutionary democracy of Russia would support the government in its attempt "to convert the revision of agreements into a *radical application* of these agreements in the direction demanded by revolutionary Russia" (italics mine).[20] Despite *Rabochaia Gazeta*'s bitter denunciation of the Allied notes, the paper claimed to find a promise to review the Allied agreements not only in the British note but also in the very vague French note, and it called for an immediate conference of representatives of the Allied governments for that purpose.[21] As might be expected, *Rech*, the organ of the Cadets and Miliukov, took an "I told you so" attitude toward what appeared to be the rapid failure of the new foreign policy.[22] Miliukov later claimed that the Allied replies revealed the bankruptcy of the foreign policy of the coalition government and the Soviet.[23]

Perhaps the editorial of the moderate socialist paper *Den* came closest to an accurate appraisal of the situation; certainly it was calmer. *Den* considered the replies of the Allies and Wilson's message to be a momentous warning to Russia that she was ceasing to be taken seriously by her Allies as a major factor in the war. The Allies spoke to democratic Russia in tones they never dared use to the Tsarist regime. Russia's demands, especially her demands for peace, were making no impression, for her army was virtually in a state of truce and she had no power to back up her demands. The Allies, *Den* argued, were unwilling to relinquish the rewards they hoped to earn from the war simply at the request of Russia, especially when she had quit fighting and there was no guarantee she would start again. Unless the situation changed, said *Den*, it was probable that "Russia will be crushed, if not on the field of battle then at the peace conference."[24]

Even as the Allied notes were arousing popular criticism and raising questions about the viability of the war aims revision policy, a related and delicate issue was also upsetting Russo-Allied relations and threatening the new foreign policy: the matter of publishing the secret treaties with the Allies outlining the spoils of war that were to fall to each country. The existence of these treaties and even something of their nature were matters of general knowledge, but they still represented a set of mysterious documents, capable of arousing strong passions. Among the newly articulate masses, a special significance was attached to them as the symbol—and perhaps the reason—for Russia's continued participation in the war. The demand that these treaties be published had been a recurrent theme in socialist newspaper editorials and in resolutions passed by local soviets, army committees, and other groups since the first days of the revolution. Miliukov had refused to do so, of course. More surprising, the Executive Committee of the Petrograd Soviet had declined to press for publication.

The Soviet leaders found themselves in a difficult position on this question. The publication of the treaties—followed by their repudiation—was seemingly in harmony with the views of the Soviet leaders on the war. Moreover, from a socialist viewpoint, making the contents known should have had the effect of arousing mass indignation against the existing order among the elements abroad that the Russians were trying to woo for Stockholm. Nevertheless, the Soviet leadership opposed publication, fearing it would lead to a rupture of the alliance to which the Tsereteli group was firmly wedded. At the All-Russian Conference of Soviets in April, Tsereteli, in answering objections to his resolution on war aims, dealt with this question. The Soviet's policy, he asserted, was not aimed at simply publishing the treaties but at having them abrogated. Premature publication of the treaties would bring down upon the Russian government not only the wrath of the imperialist governments but also that of the peoples of the Allied countries, who would not understand Russia's motives. The Russian democracy must first establish popular support for the Soviet program in other countries and find acceptance for the new war aims.[25] *Izvestiia*, commenting on Tsereteli's speech, editorialized:

The Soviet of Workers' and Soldiers' Deputies is steadfastly seeking the *abrogation* of the piratic *secret agreements*. It is striving for this goal by calling on the people of all countries to fight against their oppressors, to fight for peace without annexations or indemnities. The Soviet of Workers' and Soldiers' Deputies is striving for this goal when it takes the initiative in calling an international socialist congress.

In the not too distant future, perhaps the Soviet also will raise the question of an official abrogation of secret agreements by way of their publication. But first one must pave the way for this step in order to assure satisfactory results. The efforts of the Executive Committee are aimed in this direction (italics in original).[26]

These themes continued to be sounded during the coalition period. On May 6 *Izvestiia*, claiming a great victory for Soviet diplomacy in getting the British and French socialists to agree to participate in the Stockholm Conference, contended that this would not have been possible if Russia had published the secret treaties unilaterally. Speaking at a Menshevik conference on May 7, Tsereteli stated that to publish the secret treaties before a similar demand gained currency in other countries would create misimpressions and actually harm the cause of peace.[27] This argument was carried a step further in a postmortem by Chernov:

The one-sided publication of the secret documents of the Entente prior to the end of the war or the German Revolution, which would simultaneously expose the secrets of Wilhelm's diplomacy, it [the Soviet] regarded as a blow, not at the war as such, but only at one warring side. It meant disrupting the Entente from within, and consciously or unconsciously abetting Hohenzollern Germany.[28]

In retrospect, another, more *realpolitik* reason for the refusal of the Soviet leaders to publish the treaties unilaterally comes to mind: they wished to preserve the threat of publication to force concessions from the Russian government or the Allies. Yet there is no evidence that they ever even considered attempting to do so.

The government, quite naturally, was even more firmly opposed to the idea of publishing the treaties, also fearing a rupture in the alliance. In a press interview on May 6, immediately after taking office as Foreign Minister, Tereshchenko spoke about the widespread discussion of the question. The demands, he said, were based on humanitarian grounds but were misguided; the publication of the treaties would result in a break with the Allies and force Russia to make a separate peace.[29] There is, of course, some question of whether or not Tereshchenko really wanted to repudiate the treaties, for he never quite said so. But whatever his attitude, they were an awkward legacy from the Tsarist regime that the Provisional Government was never able to bring itself to accept completely or to repudiate totally and finally. Always a sensitive issue, the treaties remained a potential source of major embarrassment for the government, particularly if the Soviet leaders changed their minds and decided to demand their publication.*

In the face of the continued demand for publication and repudiation of the treaties and the popular outcry at what amounted to an Allied refusal to revise them, Tereshchenko was forced to make some sort of reply to the Allied notes. He seized on the vague agreements to review the treaties, and on May 31 communicated to Albert Thomas a proposal for an Allied conference to review war aims. The proposal was made public June 3. It proclaimed that the Russian revolution repre-

---

* An anecdote told by Shulgin (in Golder, *Documents*, pp. 271–72) illustrates the embarrassment created by the treaties. He asserted that on March 1, during the tumultuous first days of the revolution, Kerensky, followed by two soldiers and a man holding a bundle, suddenly burst into a meeting of the Duma Committee. Taking the bundle, he dismissed the men and threw the package on the table, with the words "Our secret treaties with the Allies. ...Hide them." Then, says Shulgin, "he disappeared as dramatically as he had appeared." The Duma Committee was in a quandary; there was no place to put the package, not even a drawer. Finally it was tossed under the table, in the hope that no one would see it there. Shulgin did not report what happened to the package afterwards. It is difficult to believe that the records of the Foreign Ministry, whose operations were not seriously disrupted during the February days, were treated so cavalierly, but Shulgin was a generally reliable observer. In any case, even this small incident— whatever was tossed under the table—illustrates the Provisional Government's discomfort over the treaties and the dilemma posed by this unhappy Tsarist heritage.

sented a radical change not only in the internal affairs of the country but also in its foreign affairs. Tereshchenko tried to paper over the growing schism with the Allies by claiming that all differences of opinion could be worked out by agreements based on the principles proclaimed by the Russian revolution. Then, ignoring the actual content and spirit of the recent Allied responses and acting as if the Allies had accepted the Russian overtures for revision of war aims, he declared:

The Russian democracy remains steadfastly loyal to the cause of the Allies, and welcomes the decision of those of the Allied powers which expressed readiness to meet the desire of the Russian Provisional Government to *reconsider* the agreements concerning the ultimate aims of the war. We suggest that there be called for the purpose a conference of representatives of Allied Powers, to take place as soon as conditions are favorable for it (italics mine).[30]

This proposal for an interallied conference was conveniently vague both about what would be done and about when the conference would meet.* It probably represented an attempt to calm socialist anger and to save at least some face after the Allies' obvious rejection of the Russian peace formula. It was hardly a serious proposal for an Allied conference. Nevertheless, the socialist press welcomed Tereshchenko's statement. *Izvestiia* called it a "decisive change in Europe's approach to international politics."[31] *Rabochaia Gazeta* stated that the note was a new step in the struggle for universal peace, which now put the burden of the struggle on the French and British people, who must force their governments to go to the Allied conference to work out a common peace platform.[32] *Rech* was caustic, referring to the proposal as a "document from the regions of revolutionary romance."[33]

The vagueness of the Tereshchenko statement was certainly in keeping with the cautious approach the Soviet leaders were taking in their relations with the Allies. Their line of thinking

---

* Tsereteli says that he helped to draft this note at Tereshchenko's request, and that the phrase "as soon as conditions are favorable for it" meant the interallied conference was to be timed with the end of the Stockholm Conference (*Vospominaniia*, I, 227–28, 370).

was clearly expressed in a pamphlet published at this time by Voitinskii, which was at one and the same time a defense of the coalition government and an explanation of its aims designed for popular consumption. Voitinskii argued that it was necessary to use circumspect language in demanding revision of war aims in order not to offend the Allies and thus make agreement on the Soviet slogan still more difficult.[34] The policy of coalition at home—of government by careful negotiation and compromise between Soviet and bourgeois leaders—had as its international counterpart a policy of careful negotiation and compromise with the bourgeois leaders of the Allied countries.

After the public proposal of June 3, the Russian government seems to have let the effort to convene an Allied conference drop for the time being. Evidently the proposal was never communicated officially or formally to the Allied governments; nor were more concrete terms about a time and place for the meeting ever announced. In a general press interview June 7, Tereshchenko was quite vague on the subject. In response to a question, he said that the proposed conference had "not yet gone beyond the stage of preliminary preparation," and that the "important question" of American participation had not yet been considered.[35] Balfour, the British Foreign Secretary, questioned about the Russian proposal in the House of Commons on June 13/26, stated that though he understood the Russian government had informed Thomas of its "intention to suggest the convocation of such a conference," no communication had been received on the matter by the British government.[36] Tereshchenko told the Russian ambassador to the United States on July 19 that no proposal had been made to the Allied governments through diplomatic channels for an interallied conference.[37]

The main reason for not proceeding with the conference was obviously the unpromising nature of the replies of the Allied governments, which did not speak well for the success of such a conference. The American, French, and Italian governments had refused to issue passports for the Stockholm Conference, and there was not yet any sign that popular support for the Russian formula was strong enough to force them to change their positions. Moreover, a great deal of trouble could be expected from the Italians, who had made extensive territorial demands the price of their participation in the war and who were not likely to give them up easily. The Russians knew this. They had intercepted a telegram from Italian Foreign Minister Sidney Sonnino to the Italian minister in Rumania stating that "the Royal Government cannot permit any revision of the treaties concluded with the Allies which might affect the advantages acquired by it by virtue of its participation in the war."[38] The Russian government, faced with the unwillingness of its Allies to revise the treaties, had little alternative but to wait until conditions were more favorable. The hope was that successful operations by the Russian army would lend authority to the voice of Russian diplomacy, and that the Soviets could stimulate more popular backing for the conference in the Allied countries. In the meantime, it was necessary to keep the matter on the diplomatic stage and to placate internal opinion by making a bold announcement of the government's intention to convoke an Allied conference. The proposal of June 3 filled both requirements. To keep it alive domestically, a series of commentaries, authorized informally by Tereshchenko, appeared in *Izvestiia* for the purpose of popularizing the government's foreign policy and war aims.[39]

Both lines of Russian foreign policy had reached an impasse by early June. The Russians believed, correctly, that the Allied rebuffs resulted in part from the growing conviction in the West that Russia was ceasing to be a major military factor in the war. Therefore the government and the Soviet turned to the possibility of restoring and demonstrating the fighting power of the army as a means of increasing the effectiveness of their diplomacy. On June 1, Tereshchenko wrote to the Russian representatives in Paris and Stockholm that the direction Russian foreign affairs took was closely linked to the condition of the army and the possibility of an offensive.[40]

The condition of the army had been dealt with in the second

section of the declaration the coalition government issued upon its formation on May 5. That section stated: "the development of its military power, both *offensive* and defensive, will constitute the most important task of the Provisional Government" (italics mine).[41] On May 14 Kerensky, as the new Minister of War, issued an order calling for discipline in the army and readiness to undertake military action. He stressed that the army was fighting for the lofty ideals of the revolution: "not a single drop of blood will be shed for a wrong cause. It is not for the sake of conquest and violence but for the sake of saving free Russia that you will go forward where your commanders and the Government lead you."[42] Kerensky then made an extended tour of the front, where he attempted to raise the morale and fighting spirit of the army in a series of personal appearances and speeches. A prominent theme of his speeches was the link between the offensive and peace, as witness the remarks he made to a Congress of the Front in Odessa on May 16: "But war and diplomacy are bound together. If you strengthen the front you strengthen the voice of diplomacy.... We prosecute the war in order to end it, and to end it quickly it is necessary to prosecute it vigorously."[43]

Kerensky's effort for an offensive was supported by all groups except the far left, and for every reason except military ones. Military and conservative groups hoped that resumption of active military operation would stop the decline of the fighting spirit of the army and bring an end to disorder in the country. If the military picture was changed, they reasoned, the political and social disintegration of Russia might be halted. It was widely felt in moderate and conservative circles that a restoration of discipline in the army would undermine the political power of the left, especially the extreme left. Indeed, if the discipline of the troops was sufficiently improved, the army might even be used to restrain the political activity of the left and thus change the general power structure in Petrograd.[44]

The Soviet leaders were not unaware of this threat and in fact constantly overrated it as a possibility; most were still looking for a counterrevolution from the right when the Bolsheviks overwhelmed them. Still, they felt that the military effectiveness of the army had to be demonstrated in order to force the Allies to pay attention to their foreign policy program. They were convinced that the Allies were discounting Russia because of the virtual truce on the Eastern front, and believed that a demonstration of military effectiveness was the only way to change this attitude. That the threat of a separate peace might be more effective was a possibility they refused to consider; they feared the effects of a separate peace above all else, believing it would ensure the triumph of Germany, which could then make Russia into a virtual colony and restore the Romanovs (generally considered by them to be the most probable sequence of events).[45] Their reasoning that a successful showing by the Russian army would lead the Allies to the peace table is clearly dubious in retrospect—it probably would have had the opposite effect. Still, the argument was plausible, and was in fact a necessary rationalization, once the Soviet leaders rejected a separate peace. Their support was in part the desperation of those without an alternative. The clamor for an offensive from both their government coalition partners and their foreign allies foreclosed the possibility of strengthening the army without launching an offensive. Indeed, it was easier to launch an offensive than to restore the army's effectiveness, as events were to prove. The Soviet leaders swallowed their doubts and hesitantly walked—or were pushed—into a gamble more likely to fail than succeed.

Various political groups, then, were led to support the idea of an offensive for different reasons. It is somewhat ironic that the left believed a successful offensive would give their foreign policy—and their domestic position—new life, while the right believed it would allow them to destroy the left. Both seemed to have ignored or forced themselves to put out of mind the question of what effect a stunning defeat (which was much more likely than a military victory) would have on their programs.

The offensive began on June 18. The Socialist press gave it a favorable but reserved and somewhat nervous reception, stressing that the main object of the revolution was still peace, even if an offensive was necessary before it could be obtained. *Rabochaia Gazeta* wrote on the 20th that, since the masses of the other warring countries had not broken away from their imperialist governments, the Russian democracy had no choice but to defend the country. If necessary, this would even include an offensive *"side by side* with the tireless struggle for peace," which could not be relaxed for a moment (italics in original). *Izvestiia* argued that there was no contradiction in the Soviet delegates arriving in Stockholm to agitate for an international socialist conference just as an offensive was launched. Only a show of Russian military might would make the Allied and enemy countries heed Russia's peace program.[46]

The nervousness exhibited by the Soviet papers was not without reason, for ominous antiwar rumblings were heard in the capital and in some army units. Signs indicating growing disenchantment, most clearly seen in the fiasco of the demonstration of June 18, were quickly confirmed. Once it became known that the offensive had started, some of the regiments in Petrograd passed resolutions opposing it, and on June 21 representatives of the Executive Committee were beaten as they were exhorting a regiment to join in the undertaking.[47] The offensive itself was a disaster. After the first push it simply disintegrated. The few effective units were destroyed in the initial battle; the others refused to fight and began to withdraw. While government and Soviet leaders watched the beginnings of a major catastrophe, the political situation in Petrograd blew up. On July 2 long-standing disagreements between the Cadet and socialist ministers came to a head over the issue of the status of the nationalities, particularly the Ukrainians, and the Cadets resigned. The next day, July 3, antiwar demonstrations by pro-Bolshevik troops, which were directed more against the Menshevik–Socialist Revolutionary leadership in the Soviet than against the government, erupted in Petrograd and quickly threatened to turn into a full revolution. Owing to a combination of poor leadership, resistance by the Soviet leaders, and charges released by the Minister of Justice to the effect that Lenin and other key Bolsheviks were agents in the pay of the German government, the uprising was quelled by July 5. The government crisis continued, however, and was intensified by the uprising. On July 7 Lvov resigned as Prime Minister and Kerensky took over as head of the government. In the meantime, on July 6, the German army reinforced the Austrians and began a counteroffensive, turning the Russian army into a disorderly mob that pillaged as it fled the front.[48]

The Soviet leaders and their associates in the government had gambled on the boost an offensive would give their diplomatic efforts. That offensive had proved disastrous beyond their greatest fears. Now government diplomacy and Soviet peace efforts were weighed down by the albatross of defeat, virtually destroying whatever prospects of success the Revolutionary Defensist program had ever had.

Collapse of Revolutionary Defensism

The failure of the June offensive, the July uprising, and the collapse of the coalition government dealt a staggering blow to both the Soviet attempt to convene an international socialist conference and the government efforts to obtain an Allied revision of war aims. These disasters undermined the government and the Soviet leaders both at home and abroad. In Russia the problem of simply holding things together in the chaos of the post-July period left little energy or opportunity for an imaginative foreign policy. There was a notable absence of fresh ideas and a distinct air of discouragement and disillusion about Russia's ability to reshape international relations or to find a way out of the war. Foreign policy and peace efforts, though no less important than before, played a less prominent role in the internal political struggle. Moreover, the unity of policy that characterized the period of the first coalition of May and June broke down. The relationship between the government and the Soviet became more ambiguous, more unstable, as the two drew further apart on policy matters.

The government crisis lasted throughout most of the month, from July 2 to the 23d. The cabinet was reshuffled after the Cadet ministers resigned on the issue of autonomy for nationality groups, but when Prince Lvov resigned July 7 over the agrarian problem, the crisis deepened, and on the 13th all the ministers put their portfolios at Kerensky's disposal. (Kerensky had become Minister-President on Lvov's resignation.) The negotiations were long and extremely complex. The Soviet leaders held to the principle of coalition. The Cadets refused, however, to participate in a new government dominated by Soviet leaders and taking its basic policy from Soviet programs. After long and futile negotiations Kerensky himself resigned on July 21. It is likely that this was a ruse by the mercurial Minister-President to bring his opponents to heel, but it might also have been a genuine gesture of frustration. In any case, the move was successful. A conference of the central committees of the major parties was convened the night of the 21st under the chairmanship of Nekrasov, the acting Minister-President. The meeting lasted until six in the morning but ended in a deadlock. The opposing parties were unable to resolve the question of whether or not the individual cabinet members should be responsible to the parties or organizations they represented. Though they were all agreed that Kerensky should be charged with forming a new government, the question remained: how much independence were he and the new government to be given?[1] Kerensky agreed on July 22 to try to form a new government. He was able to do so quickly, since most of the political parties were desperate to end the crisis.

The new cabinet was anything but strong. Obviously a creature of exigency designed to end the three-week-old government crisis, it was greeted with relief rather than enthusiasm. The direction of the new government was now firmly in the hands of the nonpartisan triumvirate of Kerensky, Tereshchenko, and Nekrasov. Nekrasov had resigned from the Cadet party on July 7, and Kerensky by now had only nominal ties with the Soviet and the Socialist Revolutionaries. The three claimed that they were above party and factional strife, that they represented the country as a whole. Though some of the new ministers were important figures in their parties, notably Chernov, Skobelev, and Avksentev, none were forceful enough to challenge the Kerensky triumvirate. Four Cadets, none of them top party leaders, were included to round out the cabinet and give it a bourgeois leaven. The very conservative *Novoe Vremia* commented, with more accuracy than it probably realized, that there was no evidence the ministers Kerensky had summoned to save the revolution would prove equal to such heroic action.[2]

Probably the most notable feature of the new government was the absence of Tsereteli. His nonparticipation in the new government is difficult to explain. Without question, if he had wanted to be included, he could have had any post he desired. The fact is, he had categorically declared at the outset of the negotiations to form the new government that he planned to return entirely to Soviet work.[3] There is very little commentary, then or since, on the reasons for his decision. *Rech*, remarking that his absence was "the first thing to strike the eye about the new list of ministers," offered no reasons for his departure or speculation on its cause.[4] Nevertheless, some reasons can be inferred from his general attitude and the political situation at the time. Tsereteli had entered the government unwillingly in May and perhaps sought an opportunity to leave as soon as possible. Nor can one discount the possibility that he realized what a weak instrument the new government would be and wanted no part of it. A statement attributed to him by one close observer clearly indicates an aversion to government membership: "What would be the sense; just another reputation destroyed."[5] Then, too, after the July days Tsereteli had served temporarily as Minister of the Interior, and thus had partial responsibility for the repressive actions against the Bolsheviks, army deserters, and other dissident elements. Though less squeamish about such action than most of his socialist colleagues, he shared the general socialist dislike of repressivse measures—at least against ordinary soldiers and fellow socialists. Also, his health probably played a role. He had been in ill health for many years, and the strain and pace of events in 1917 taxed his strength. His health may already have been nearing the breaking point that was to force him to take leave of politics and go to the Caucasus for a rest just before the Bolshevik revolution. Probably the most important reason, however, was his desire to concentrate his efforts on the affairs of the Soviet, where the Menshevik–Socialist Revolutionary bloc had been shaken by the July events. This was the explanation he himself gave in a speech explaining his resignation to the Executive Committee.[6] There were, then, a number of factors that undoubtedly entered into Tsereteli's decision to leave the cabinet.

In any event, the end of the cabinet crisis did not bring political stability; the political situation remained very fluid and highly charged. Although the Bolshevik leaders were in hiding and the party seemingly discredited, the party organization survived the half-hearted repressive measures of the government and soon began to rebuild. The success of the effort was evident in a new growth of support among the delegates to the Petrograd Soviet and among the district soviets in Petrograd, where in August the Bolsheviks made their first significant inroads since early June. Meanwhile there was also a revival of activity on the political right, marked by a call for "restoration of order" and the search for a "man on horseback" to save Russia. Such a man seemed to appear in the person of Gen. Lavr Kornilov, the new Supreme Commander. Not only did Kornilov stand as the champion of a firm hand in the army and elsewhere; he had a personal score to settle with the Soviet leaders, dating from his humiliation during the April Crisis when, as commander of the Petrograd garrison, his orders had been countermanded by the Soviet. A gathering test of strength was clearly evident at the Moscow State Conference of August 12–15. Called by Kerensky to demonstrate the unity of all the political, social, and economic forces of the country with the government, it revealed exactly the opposite. The pro-Soviet and pro-Kornilov forces separated into two hostile camps.[7] In a situation where all attention was focused on the political struggle and the Kornilovite demand for discipline and order, foreign affairs were virtually ignored. Tereshchenko was not even among the ministers who reported to the conference, and the Soviet speakers touched on foreign affairs only in passing.

During this long period of governmental weakness and uncertainty the international position of the Provisional Government slipped even lower. On July 8 the reshuffled government had issued a statement that reaffirmed the policy statement of May 5, when the coalition government was formed. Though it stressed the government's determination to defend the country, it also reiterated the need to convince the army that it was fighting for purely democratic goals. The new statement declared that the Russian government intended to invite the Allies to hold a conference in August "to coordinate their actions in carrying out the principles proclaimed by the Russian revolution." Soviet as well as Foreign Ministry delegates would represent Russia.[8] This declaration, like that of June 3, seems to have been a sop to public opinion rather than an announcement of an action that was in fact to be carried through. Tereshchenko was well aware that there was little likelihood the Allies would agree to such a conference, considering recent events. Moreover, he realized that given Russia's weakness, this was no time for a revision of the treaties, as witness his statement to the Russian ambassador in Washington, B. A. Bakhmetev, on July 11/24: "in view of the latest events at the front and the situation in the country, I deem it necessary to postpone somewhat the proposed conference and, *suspending for the time being all negotiations with respect to future peace conditions*, to concentrate all our attention on the continuance of the war" (italics mine).[9] This theme—concentration on the war effort—was to loom ever larger in official Russian thinking in the coming months; it represented a distinct shift of emphasis in foreign policy.

At the same time Tereshchenko was pacifying domestic opinion, he had to attempt to assure the Allies that recent events and the government's new proclamation did not mean Russia's collapse, and that she had no intention of withdrawing from the war. In a message sent to the Allies on July 19, he talked not of peace and war aims but of defense of the country. Though he referred enigmatically to continuing "the war until the final triumph of the principles proclaimed by the Russian Revolution," the general emphasis of the note, which even mentioned preparation for new offensives, was on war.[10] Clearly, this was no time to speak to the Allies of making peace. Rather, they must be persuaded that Russia's defeat at the front and internal turmoil would not cause her to abandon the struggle or move toward a separate peace.

Tereshchenko's assurances notwithstanding, the Allies began to reconsider Russia's role in the war. Instructive of the impact of the July events are two memorandums drawn up by the French General Staff in preparation for an Allied conference that was to meet in Paris July 11–13/24–26. One was written on July 8/21 and assumed considerable continued Russian military contribution to the war. It was replaced by July 11/24 by another that included planning for the military strategy to be followed if Russian defection or inaction were to release large numbers of German troops for use on the Western front; indeed the final version seemed to assume such developments in the near future.[11] The difference is easily accounted for: on July 8/21 the Russian offensive was still believed to be underway; but by the time the conference convened, news had been received of the Russian rout following the German counteroffensive and of the deepening political crisis following Prince Lvov's resignation. The British reaction was much the same: on July 18/31 the War Cabinet discussed the military and diplomatic alternatives if Russia were to defect or become totally worthless militarily.[12]

Indicative of the way in which Russian influence and prestige had fallen was the treatment accorded Russia at another Allied conference, this one held in London on July 25–26/August 7–8. On the morning of the first day of the conference, the Russian chargé in London, Konstantin Nabokov, called the Foreign Office seeking an interview with Balfour in connection with new information received from Petrograd. To his surprise he was told that the Foreign Secretary was busy with the inter-allied conference then meeting and would not be able to receive callers for three days. Nabokov told his unwitting informant that the Russian representative found it most interesting to discover that an Allied conference was meeting, Russia being one of the Allies. A few minutes later Nabokov received an invitation to attend the conference. When he arrived, Alexandre Ribot, the French Prime Minister–Foreign Minister; Paul Painlevé, the French Minister of War; Albert Thomas; Marshal

Foch; Sidney Sonnino, the Italian Premier; Guglielmo Imperiali, the Italian Ambassador to London; the entire British cabinet; and others were already assembled. Nabokov was forced to sit through a long discussion over whether a strong protest should be sent to the Russian government about the continued disorders, and then through the drafting and approval of such a message.* It was not in fact a "strong protest"; still it was offensive to the Russians by its very existence.[13] Only days earlier the War Cabinet, looking forward to the Allied conference, had discussed whether to invite the Russian military representative, General Dessino, deciding that if they did it would be difficult not to include the Serbians and the Rumanians. How Russia's status had fallen! Nabokov's attendance was discussed also, but there is no indication in the records of the meeting of the final decision.[14] In any case, neither was invited. Dessino himself wrote earlier, in May: "It is too bad we are so good to their [British] representatives in Russia; they certainly are not to ours."[15]

The Russian reaction to such treatment is not hard to imagine. Kerensky's temper flared occasionally at the continued advice from the Allies on how to govern Russia.[16] ("How would Lloyd George like it if a Russian were to come tell him how to manage the English people?" he asked one British representative.)[17] Popular hostility toward the Allies mounted from July on, despite the repression of the Bolsheviks and the temporary closing of their presses following the July days, which either removed altogether or sharply curtailed the most outspoken organs of expression. The sentiment against the Allies was especially strong among the soldiers, who increasingly shifted their support to the more radical parties. On August 6 two Rumanian

---

* The proposal to send such a message came in part from the British, in response to telegrams from Buchanan and the military attaché, General Barter. Barter telegraphed August 4 (July 22): "Socialists want to run a class war in preference to the race war, and this appeals to the mass of the soldiers as being less dangerous. Tseretelli and others think they can run both wars simultaneously. We have to tell Russian Government plainly that this is impossible" (Great Britain, War Cabinet minutes, No. 205, Aug. 7 [July 25], Cab. 23/3).

military attachés were set upon and arrested by a drunken soldier-member of the Soviet because they were speaking French in a street car.[18] Gorky's *Novaia Zhizn* printed a series of articles so insulting to the Allies that the government found it necessary to instruct the Minister of Justice to draw up a law to stop such invective in the press.[19] Tereshchenko asked Buchanan to reciprocate by inducing the English journalists in Russia to stop sending reports that might arouse anti-Russian feeling in England.[20] Neither effort succeeded.

During the July-August period Tereshchenko took on more of the coloration of the traditional Russian Foreign Minister, attempting to safeguard Russia's international position and interests within the trying context of military defeat, domestic turmoil, and strained relations with the Allies. He recognized that the situation called for a generally passive role in international affairs. Nevertheless, events forced him to be active, some of them arising directly out of the earlier policies of the government and the Soviet. Particularly troublesome from the Russian point of view were a series of Allied meetings on Asia Minor, the Balkans, and the conduct of the war. Russia was represented at some of these meetings, at others not, but at no time did she have an authoritative spokesman present. In any case there was a tendency on the part of the Allies to ignore Russian interests that Tereshchenko found difficult to counter.

The Russians were especially bothered by the Allied decisions and actions concerning Asia Minor and Greece. In the case of Asia Minor, both the national interests of Russia and the Soviet peace program were endangered. The Italian government continually prodded the French and British to draw up new agreements dividing the Turkish empire, at the same time requesting permission to make a statement in the Italian parliament about Italy's expected gains. Tereshchenko energetically opposed such actions, both because of the uproar it would create in Petrograd and because an expanded Italian sphere of domination in Asia Minor ran counter to traditional Russian interests in the Straits area. Thanks to Tereshchenko's opposition, plus

British reluctance to force the issue, no settlement was ever reached.[21] The maneuvering, however, led Tereshchenko further and further from the Soviet peace slogan and more and more along the path of traditional diplomacy. He adroitly managed to avoid publicly or privately committing himself to either endorsing or renouncing the annexations promised Russia in the secret treaties, no small achievement under the circumstances.

The Balkans and particularly Greece were another source of irritation in the relations between Russia and the Allies, and another issue with great consequences for both the Soviet peace formula and traditional Russian interests. The Allies had intervened in Greek politics to ensure a government friendly to them, and had even opened a front in Salonika, the soil of a neutral, Greece. The Russians' apprehensions over increasing French influence in Greece led them to take a dim view of these proceedings. Tereshchenko protested the Franco-British action in deposing King Constantine for a more pliable government, not only because the action was offensive in itself but also because the new regime was favorable to Greek expansionism, including the annexation of Constantinople. The Russian protests were ignored. Though the Allied actions did not arouse enormous popular protest in Russia, the reaction was still such that Tereshchenko felt a public statement was called for: Russia had opposed the action, he declared, and she would attempt to get the Russian formula of national self-determination applied to the final settlement of the Greek question.[22]

Potentially much more explosive domestically than the disputes over Asia Minor and Greece was the issue raised by the Russian revolutionaries—the publication of the secret treaties. This continued to be an emotional question, but fortunately for the government, just as the question became most dangerous internationally, other issues arose that diverted domestic opinion. The question of making the contents of the treaties public became an international issue in July, when the new German Chancellor, Georg Michaelis, discussed the annexationist views of the Entente in a press statement. Michaelis challenged Ribot to deny that a treaty had been signed in Petrograd during the interallied conference in February 1917 giving France territory on the east bank of the Rhine. He also mentioned the planned French annexation of Syria and the Asia Minor agreements between France, Russia, and England. He made some mistakes, but his factual information, together with his direct challenge to Ribot, were enough to force Ribot to make a reply. Michaelis' statement contained gross inaccuracies and misrepresentations, Ribot asserted to the Chamber of Deputies on July 18/31, and as for the letters that had been exchanged between Paris and Petrograd: "Whenever the Russian Government is willing to publish these letters we have no objection."[23]

Ribot's statement was extremely embarrassing to the Russian government, which had rejected internal demands for the publication of the treaties on the grounds that the Allies would object. Tereshchenko instructed the Russian chargé in Paris to inform Ribot that the Russian government had no objection to the publication of the notes exchanged in February 1917, by which France had been given a free hand to determine her eastern border.* However, he pointed out, in maintaining the demands made in February regarding her eastern border, France would cause an unfavorable impression in "Russian democratic circles." If, in view of this consideration, Ribot felt it best not to publish the agreement, Tereshchenko asked that he make a new public statement to that effect.[24] The matter was allowed to rest there.

Fortunately for the Russian government, the socialist press did not pursue the issue. At the time of the Michaelis-Ribot exchange, Russia was in the midst of the deep and prolonged ministerial crisis, and little attention was paid to their statements. *Izvestiia* made no mention of Ribot's speech, and although *Delo Naroda* carried both Michaelis' statement and Ribot's rebuttal, including Ribot's remarks about the publica-

---

* His telegram mistakenly refers to the western border of France. The same agreement had given Russia a free hand in redrawing *her* western border.

tion of the letters, it ignored the publication issue in an editorial on the statements a day later.[25] Possibly the Soviet leaders felt it best to let the matter pass, lest they work themselves into an awkward position. However, their opponents were not inclined to let them off so easily. Iu. O. Martov, for instance, denounced the Soviet leaders for their inaction on the front page of *Novaia Zhizn*,[26] which followed up his attack with several editorials. However, popular attention was directed elsewhere, and nothing came of it.

But Ribot did not let the matter drop. He was under strong pressure at home about the secret treaties as the aroused Chamber of Deputies pressed for more details.* Finally, on September 6/19 he made another statement in the Chamber on the subject. He was ready at any time to produce the treaties, but he had to consider the desires of the Allies: "It is from Petrograd that the request reached me to defer publication."[27] This was an extremely free interpretation, no doubt intentionally so, of Tereshchenko's statement. After a lengthy and somwhat confused exchange of notes, Tereshchenko finally instructed M. M. Sevastopulo, the Russian chargé in Paris, to clear up the situation once and for all by declaring officially to the French government that the Russian government had no objection "to making public all the agreements in general, concluded either prior to or during the war, provided the consent of the other interested Allies is obtained."[28] This was a strong statement, and it placed the responsibility for publication squarely on Ribot's shoulders. The qualification "provided the consent of the other interested Allies is obtained" was an important one, however. Since they were involved in every agreement except the one made in February, their consent would have to be secured, and as Tere-

---

* On August 25/September 7, Ribot was forced to resign. A major factor in his rejection was the discontent of the Socialists over his refusal to issue passports for Stockholm. On August 30/September 13, a government was formed by Painlevé, Ribot's Minister of War, but Ribot continued to hold a cabinet post, assuming the position of Foreign Minister. As a result the Socialist Party refused to participate in the government for the first time since the outbreak of the war.

shchenko admitted in this same telegram, it was not likely that either Rumania or Italy would agree to their publication. Sevastopulo delivered a note to the French government on September 18/October 1 that embodied the Tereshchenko statement, and the matter evidently ended there. Tereshchenko had successfully extracted himself from a difficult situation without giving up anything or bringing on a domestic crisis.

An extremely interesting feature of this exchange was the revelation that Tereshchenko was unwilling formally to relinquish the Straits. In one telegram Sevastopulo had reported that Ribot felt the Asia Minor agreements "stood apart" from the agreement on Constantinople and the Straits, meaning that the agreements on Asia Minor could not be considered for publication, since they were not yet completed. Tereshchenko, however, took this to mean that Ribot did not consider the fulfillment of the Asia Minor treaties to be dependent on the fulfillment of the Straits agreement. Tereshchenko heatedly replied on September 12/25 that this interpretation was unacceptable. Citing the provision in the original agreement that Russia's assent to the partition of Asia Minor depended on the execution of the Straits agreement, he concluded: "it follows that the Asia Minor agreement cannot be considered apart from the agreement about Constantinople and the Straits, and that any change in the latter will unavoidably affect, in one way or another, the former."[29] Tereshchenko wanted assurances that the Straits agreement would be operative if Russia so desired, and that she could, if she wished, annul the Asia Minor agreements by repudiating the Straits agreement. By autumn, he was as determined as Miliukov had been in the spring that Russia's option to annex Constantinople and the Straits would remain in force, should she want to exercise it after the war. His actions would indicate that he was moving further away from the Soviet position and abandoning the stance of a "new diplomacy" in favor of traditional policies and methods.

To fully evaluate Tereshchenko's apparent shift in policy, one has to consider the concurrent fate of the Soviet's efforts to convene the Stockholm Conference. The Soviet was as heavily handicapped by the disasters of July as the Foreign Ministry was, perhaps more so. Whereas Tereshchenko preferred to mark time, waiting to see how the situation developed at home and abroad, the Soviet leaders pressed forward with increasingly desperate efforts to convoke an international socialist conference. The July-August period witnessed the end of their hopes.

An important part of the effort to convene the conference was the Soviet delegation that was sent to Stockholm and then on to Western Europe in June. The organization of the delegation was delayed for some weeks in the late spring and early summer because of the Soviet leaders' preoccupation with pressing day-to-day problems and their desire to await the convening of the All-Russian Congress of Soviets, which could give the delegation more authority. The delay reduced the delegation's effectiveness, for it did not reach Western Europe until July, when the unrest that might have provided support for a negotiated peace was declining. A five-man delegation finally departed for Stockholm in mid-June. Three members, I. P. Goldenberg, V. N. Rozanov, and A. N. Smirnov, all Social Democrat adherents of the Menshevik–Socialist Revolutionary ruling bloc in the Soviet, arrived on June 19; N. S. Rusanov, the single Socialist Revolutionary on the delegation, and G. M. Erlikh (Henryk Erlich), a Bundist, arrived the following day. The delegates had a fairly broad mandate: they were to talk with all groups and to take whatever steps would further the cause of the conference as long as they did not make any agreements that would limit the freedom of the Russian delegation to the conference itself. They were to try to get the various groups and factions to agree to participate in the conference with as few preconditions as possible, and to try to get advance agreement that its decisions would be binding on all participants.[30]

On its arrival in Stockholm the delegation immediately began talks with both the International Socialist Committee, representing the far left in European socialism as organized at the Zimmerwald Conference in 1915, and the Dutch-Scandinavian

Committee. Talks with the first proved fruitless, for its members insisted on excluding the Majority parties from any socialist conference. Discussions with the Dutch-Scandinavian Committee, however, were more satisfactory, though there were significant differences of opinion on some important questions, the same ones that had plagued the Soviet's discussions with the Allied socialists: should conference decisions be binding on all participants, as the Russians desired, and should the question of responsibility for starting the war be put on the agenda, as advocated by the pro-Ally socialists, which the Russians opposed. There were other, less important differences as well, but generally the talks were harmonious. On June 29/July 11 the two groups merged to form the Russian-Dutch-Scandinavian Committee and issued a call for a general socialist conference, to convene August 15/28. At the same time, the Soviets also met with representatives of various European socialist parties.[31] The optimism generated by the success of these early efforts is revealed in a letter from Rozanov to Chkheidze on June 27/July 8: "The authority of the Soviet is enormous. It was enough for one paper to write that I am your right-hand man in international politics (I do not pretend to be so), and everyone began to turn to me: 'End the war—this is in your power.' "[32]

The major obstacle to the conference was the opposition of the French and British Majority, and so the Russians went on to Western Europe to persuade them to support the conference. They arrived in England on July 15/28, the very day that Arthur Henderson returned from his trip to Russia. By that time their position had been made more difficult and their optimism undermined by news of the series of July disasters in Russia.[33] If these events weakened Russia's prestige and bargaining power—and consequently the prestige and bargaining power of the delegation—they certainly heightened the delegates' awareness of the importance of the success of their mission. The meetings with the British Labour Party were friendly, but the old disagreements quickly arose, especially over the question of making the decisions of the conference binding on the participants, a stipulation the British strongly opposed. Nevertheless, the Labour Party Executive Committee, at the urging of Henderson, who had been converted to the cause of Stockholm during his Russian visit, declared its support for the Stockholm Conference. This was a significant victory.[34]

The Russian delegation, accompanied by several top British Labour Party leaders, quickly moved on to France for meetings with the French Socialist Party and to woo French opinion. While there, they met with some parliamentary groups as well. These meetings were critical, for the French government had already declared itself against Stockholm. At a meeting with the Foreign Affairs Commissions of the Senate and the Chamber of Deputies, the delegates explained their position. Russia would not make a separate peace, they assured their listeners (much to the Frenchmen's relief), but she desperately needed peace. Goldenberg put the problem succinctly: "The revolution will kill the war, or the war will kill the revolution, and that is why we seek peace."[35] During their stay in France, the delegates were feted by various other groups—and were roundly attacked by the conservative press.

The meetings with the French socialists were difficult but essentially successful. The French were insistent that the question of war guilt be the first item on the agenda of the Stockholm Conference. The Russians were adamantly opposed to this, arguing that this question would immediately break up the conference. Finally a compromise was worked out: the issue was to be put under the general agenda heading "The World War and the International." As for the question of the binding nature of the conference, it was agreed that each party at the conference would make a public statement about how it intended to implement the conference's resolutions. The Russians, for their part, had to agree to move the conference back to September 9/August 26, so that an interallied Socialist conference and some national conferences could meet before Stockholm.[36] The successes in Paris were followed by a trip to Italy that promised to be even more successful, when suddenly events took a turn for the worse.

While the delegates were soliciting support on the continent, a major conflict developed in London between Henderson and the British War Cabinet on the issue of Stockholm. On July 13/26 Henderson told the War Cabinet that if the Stockholm Conference met, as he was convinced it would, it was his duty to go.[37] He was determined to win the Labour Party's approval when it met on July 28/August 10, and there was little doubt that he would be able to do so. Lloyd George and the War Cabinet, meanwhile, had shifted from their position of April and May, when they had approved of the conference, or at least tolerated it. Lloyd George now opposed the conference, and he was supported by his fellow cabinet members, especially the Conservatives led by Lord Curzon and Bonar Law. At a meeting on July 17/30 the War Cabinet decided that "it was not now desirable for Britain to be represented at Stockholm."[38] A number of reasons might be adduced for this change of attitude. First, the failure of the Russian offensive and the July crisis had tarnished the Stockholm effort, along with other Russian foreign policies, and it no longer seemed so important to humor the Soviet.[39] Second, by late summer it was becoming obvious that the German submarine offensive would not be effective; consequently, the possibility of Britain being forced by this weapon into a negotiated peace receded. Third, Lloyd George had by this time talked with the French and Italian leaders, whose governments had refused passports, and they had urged him to take a similar stand. Fourth, public opinion in England seemed to be against the idea of English citizens of any political creed meeting with Germans, and Lloyd George was a politician who kept a close check on the public pulse. Simply put, the Soviets failed to stimulate the ground swell of public opinion that might have forced the governments to change their policy.[40] Finally, the attitude of the Russian government played a role in the British decision, this by way of a major dispute that threatened to upset both the Kerensky government and British-Russian relations.

The Russian chargé d'affaires in London, Konstantin Nabokov, an ardent advocate of the policy of total defeat of Germany, strongly opposed the Stockholm Conference, which he saw as a German maneuver to avoid the consequences of certain defeat. On July 21/August 3 he telegraphed Tereshchenko, expressing concern that Russian governmental support for the conference was undermining "the closeness of our union with Great Britain," and requesting permission to declare to Foreign Secretary Balfour "that the Russian Government as well as His Majesty's Government regard this matter [Stockholm] as a party concern and not as a matter of state, and that the decisions of the Conference, should it be convened, would in no way be binding on the future course of Russian policy and of Russia's relations with her Allies."[41] This seemed a fairly harmless statement, merely reflecting the actual legal status of the conference, and an easy way to smooth relations with Britain, for Nabokov had implied that Balfour requested such a statement. On July 27/August 9, the day before the Labour Party conference convened, the desired response was received from Tereshchenko:

I entirely approve of the declaration to be made to his Majesty's Government in the sense suggested by you, and you are hereby authorized to inform the Secretary of State for Foreign Affairs that although the Russian Government does not deem it possible to prevent Russian delegates from taking part in the Stockholm Conference, they regard this Conference as a party concern and its decisions in no wise binding upon the liberty of actions of the Government.*

Nabokov immediately sent his telegraph and Tereshchenko's reply to Balfour, with a covering note. He was placing this before the British government, he stated in the note, in order to counter the prevailing impression in England that Russia ardently desired the Stockholm Conference, an argument that was being used to persuade the Labour Party conference to vote in

* There are some important variations between the English and Russian language versions of Nabokov's memoirs, including the addition or omission of whole passages. This wording appears in the English version (C. Nabokoff, *Ordeal of a Diplomat*, p. 137). The Russian word *vospretit'* (in *Ispytaniia diplomata*, p. 118) might be better translated "to prohibit" rather than "to prevent," which makes Tereshchenko's position sound more legalistic. Nabokov's choice of English words indicates stronger opposition but helplessness, which was the connotation he wanted to convey—and probably an expression of his own feelings.

favor of Stockholm.[42] Here Nabokov gave a slight but significant twist to Tereshchenko's telegram, which reflected a change of attitude on the part of the Russian government since July, when it had given full support to Stockholm, but which certainly did not repudiate the conference. In it, Tereshchenko dealt only with the legal position of the conference and its members, not with the desirability of the conference, a question that he did not raise explicitly. Whether the Russian government favored, disapproved, or was neutral toward the conference was not specified; all the government clearly indicated was that it would not take steps to prevent the conference being held. Nabokov went further, however, implying in his note that the Russian government did not favor the conference and perhaps even opposed it, and by inference attributing that meaning to Tereshchenko's message.

Balfour gave the Russian statements to Lloyd George. The cabinet had already tentatively decided on July 25/August 7 not to grant passports for the conference. Now Lloyd George and his fellow cabinet members found a useful weapon that could be used to justify their own position and to beat down the Labourites and Henderson. The impression of the Nabokov and Tereshchenko statements was reinforced by a telegram from Albert Thomas to Lloyd George on July 28/August 10, which stated that Kerensky and the government did not want the conference to meet. The War Cabinet formally decided against issuing passports for Stockholm the same day.[43] Lloyd George forwarded the Nabokov and Tereshchenko statements to Henderson, indicating that Henderson would want to use them in his speech before the Labour Party.[44]

Henderson, however, did not use the material in his speech. In the course of a powerful argument for attendance at Stockholm, he did state that the Russian government appeared to have modified its views on the conference somewhat, but apart from this, he ignored the notes, possibly because they were unfavorable to his position if the Nabokov interpretation was accepted. More likely, however, he read Tereshchenko's message

for the careful balancing act that it was, and dismissed Nabokov's note as the unimportant comments of a person who had
little knowledge of, and less influence on, Petrograd politics.
Having recently returned from Petrograd, Henderson well knew
that the Stockholm Conference was extremely popular, that it
was regarded by many as the last hope for the salvation of Russia and the revolution, and that if in theory it was a "party concern," in fact it was of necessity accepted by the government.
What he did not fully appreciate was that events had moved at
such a pace in Russia since his visit as to make pre-July impres-
sions no longer reliable.

The Labour Conference voted in favor of Stockholm, much
to the outrage of Lloyd George, who vowed that Henderson
must leave the cabinet.[45] Henderson was subjected to intense
abuse in the papers, which were strongly prowar. He was denounced as a scoundrel, a traitor, and all the other epithets that
are hurled at a man who takes an unpopular stand on such an
emotional subject as negotiated peace in time of all-out war.
On July 29/August 11 he submitted his resignation to Lloyd
George.

The Russian messages were made public when Lloyd George
released them for publication, along with Henderson's resignation and his own comments on Henderson's actions. Nabokov
had given him permission to do so without first clearing the
matter with Tereshchenko. However, realizing the impropriety
of his action, he asked that the source of the information not be
given—as if Tereshchenko would not know—and later he expressed anxiety about his position as a consequence.[46] Nabokov's request is one reason Lloyd George's statement did not dis-
tinguish Nabokov's note from that of the Russian government
other than to refer to the one as the "covering note,"[47] although
the obscurity certainly suited Lloyd George's purpose too. Meanwhile, Kerensky's supposed view, as expressed in Thomas's telegram, became public during a debate in the House of Commons
on Henderson's resignation.[48] Henderson, who had not seen the
Thomas telegram but had been informed by a member of the

French embassy that Kerensky opposed the conference, referred in his speech to Kerensky's opposition and mistakenly attributed the telegram to him. Lloyd George did not correct this error in his own speeches, as he certainly should have, Kerensky being the Prime Minister of an Allied country. Thus the impression was given publicly that Kerensky not only opposed the conference but had personally so informed Lloyd George. Kerensky thus joined Miliukov and Tereshchenko, becoming the third Russian minister to get caught up in domestic troubles because an Allied politician had furthered his own ambitions at a Russian colleague's expense. As for Thomas, it is difficult to tell whether his action in sending the telegram, like his earlier involvement in Miliukov's fall, should be termed machination, meddling, or fumbling!*

The Russian socialists were appalled when the Russian messages appeared in the press. Their confusion was the more complete because it was not clear that there were three separate items: the Thomas telegram about Kerensky, the Tereshchenko telegram, and the Nabokov note.[49] The Soviet delegates, who had hurried to London from Rome, telegraphed Petrograd for an explanation when the news first became public in London. On August 2 the Russian government issued a public denial: the government had always maintained that the conference was a party affair and its decisions were therefore not binding on the government, the right to resolve questions of war and peace being the prerogative of the governments of the Allied countries. Nevertheless, the Russian government had always held that an exchange of views such as that planned for Stockholm would be beneficial, and both Kerensky and Tereshchenko had informed the Allied governments that they considered it undesirable to place obstacles in the path of the conference.[50]

---

* Evidently, like Lloyd George, Thomas had come full circle and now opposed the conference, at least privately. Publicly he was equivocal, but the policy he proposed would in effect wreck the conference. Speaking in Paris on July 30/August 12, he stated that the Stockholm Conference would not bring peace, and that the purpose in going was to get the International to condemn the German Social Democrats for their support of the German government. See *The Times* (London), August 15(2), p. 5.

Tereshchenko went further the next day. After repeating in essence the previous statement, he explained that his telegram had been in response to one from Nakobov. As for the letter to which Lloyd George referred, it had been written by Nabokov, and the Foreign Ministry had not yet seen its contents. Kerensky, he emphasized, had not sent any message at all.[51] At the same time Tereshchenko reprimanded Nabokov and ordered him to confine himself to transmitting the exact texts of government declarations "on political questions of principle."[52]

The statements from the government soothed the indignant Russian socialist press. *Izvestiia*'s editorial following Tereshchenko's speech was all but an audible sigh of relief: the statement of the Foreign Minister, said *Izvestiia*, "undoubtedly will bring calm to the midst of the revolutionary democracy," and reinforced the democracy's confidence that the Provisional Government was continuing to carry out its avowed foreign policy aims.[53] *Rabochaia Gazeta* carried a similar editorial.[54] *Rech* was also happy to see the statements of the government and the Foreign Minister, but for a different reason. *Rech* claimed that the government's position indicated it was finally making an effort to emancipate itself from the tutelage of the Soviet. As for Tereshchenko's statement, the paper noted his declaration that Stockholm was a party affair and that the government had the final voice in making peace. After three months, *Rech* said caustically, he finally had found the proper tone of a Russian Foreign Minister.[55]

The exact roles of Tereshchenko and Kerensky in this affair are difficult to assess, as is their general attitude toward Stockholm at this time. The available evidence indicates that both men—and Tereshchenko for certain—privately opposed the conference by this time but wavered in their opposition. Kerensky's attitude is especially difficult to establish because the evidence is indirect. According to a July 31 dispatch from Buchanan to the Foreign Office, both Tereshchenko and Kerensky had privately admitted to him that they would rather the conference did not meet, but did not want their views to be made public. Nevertheless, wrote Buchanan, Kerensky, on being informed of the publication of the Tereshchenko-Nabokov correspondence, had begged him to urge the British government not to refuse passports to the socialists.[56] The background to the Thomas message "Kerensky does not wish the conference" is complex. Konstantin Nabokov states in his memoirs that though the origins were a mystery to him at the time, Tereshchenko later told him that Kerensky had expressed his opposition to the conference in a private conversation, and that he, Tereshchenko, had reported this in confidence to Eugène Pettit of the French embassy in Petrograd, who was a close friend of Thomas.[57] If this was indeed the origin of Thomas's information, it took a rather circuitous route. Moreover, the role assigned Tereshchenko is striking, for he surely must have known that Pettit would not keep the information "confidential." Tereshchenko probably did not expect the information to be made public but did expect it to be transmitted to the French government, where it might bolster French and British governmental opposition to the conference.

Tereshchenko's attitude is much clearer than Kerensky's and the evidence more direct. The Pettit leak indicates Tereshchenko's growing opposition to the conference and the methods he resorted to in order to sabotage it. On August 5, two days after his press statement on the Nabokov affair, he sent a telegram to Bakhmetev in Washington in which he stated that though he thought the conference probably would meet, "in the present circumstance I personally disapprove of the Stockholm Conference."[58] This is certainly explicit! More indirect testimony comes from Marquis Carlotti, the Italian ambassador to Russia, who on August 17/30 reported to his government an exchange between Tereshchenko and the French ambassador. In the first place, Tereshchenko reportedly said, it was desirable that the conference never meet, since it would be impossible for the government to avoid being influenced by the decisions taken there.[59] There is no direct evidence to show why Tereshchenko came to oppose the conference so strongly. He was, however, very jealous of the prerogatives of his office, and whatever his feelings about the need for peace, he may have desired above all to get rid of this competing force. His diplomatic dispatches emphasized—quite correctly, to be sure—that only the government had the right to decide peace terms and to make peace. Still, he never expressed himself against the principle or desirability of a negotiated peace.

Both Kerensky and Tereshchenko, then, seem to have taken an anti-Stockholm position by late summer. Given their concern with strengthening the government, this is certainly understandable. Both were jealous of the government's prerogatives and were making a general effort to free themselves not only from Soviet but also from party tutelage. It was in this period that they proclaimed themselves above party and strove to establish a government whose members would not be responsible to political parties or the Soviet. The failure of the conference would undermine the prestige of the Soviet, thus weakening the government's chief rival in all phases of activity, especially foreign affairs. A weaker Soviet would, perhaps, release the government from that "house arrest" Shulgin had derided. Also, during July and August there was a slight swing to the right in political attitudes in Petrograd, a reaction to the July uprising. The government acted more independently of the Soviet than at any previous time. The Soviet was still a powerful force, and it could not be flouted publicly with impunity, but it might more readily be subverted privately.

By early August the Stockholm Conference was dying a lingering death. The effort still limped along, and hope was not totally abandoned, but the more realistic members of the Soviet leadership realized that the conference would not meet, at least not in the near future. Despite the support of the British Labour Party, the decision of the British cabinet not to grant passports sealed the conference's fate. Now all the Allied governments had set themselves against it, and even the attitude of the Russian government had been called into question.

At the same time the precarious and hard-won unity of the Allied socialists was collapsing under this pressure and public apathy. An interallied socialist conference met in London on August 15–16/28–29, with the Soviet delegation in attendance. After long and futile debates, the representatives failed to reach an agreement on a draft of peace terms and split into two quarreling factions, as a number of Majority socialists defected from the pro-Stockholm camp.[60] The attempt to create a united Allied socialist front on Stockholm as a means of forcing the Allied governments to move toward peace ended in a complete disaster. The Soviet delegates had been fairly successful in swinging moderate socialist support for Stockholm at first, but they could not influence or even deal directly with the Allied governments. Indeed, as disorder spread in Russia and the weakness of the Menshevik–Socialist Revolutionary coalition they represented became apparent, their ability to influence even the labor and socialist parties declined. The delegation made its weary way back to Stockholm, where it joined in issuing one last defiant proclamation of faith that the meeting would take place, and then in September returned home to a disintegrating Russia.

The main hope of the Soviet leaders had been that the prestige of the revolution and the Soviet would result in, first, the Allied socialist parties and, then, the Allied governments accepting the program and leadership of the Soviet in the search for peace. But the Soviet was unable to force its program, beyond general principles, even on the Allied socialists. As *Izvestiia* ruefully admitted on August 26, the attempt to obtain an immediate peace had been unsuccessful, and the Soviet could not in the near future count on the peoples of Western Europe for support in the struggle for peace. A report from the Soviet delegation in London put it more bluntly: "The possibility of convoking the International in the near future is negligible."[61] By the end of August the wave of war-weariness that had swept Europe in the spring and early summer had receded, destroying the emotional foundations on which the Soviet leaders had planned to build. The Allied socialists equivocated, the Allied governments set themselves against a negotiated peace, and even the Russian government seemed to be disassociating itself from the effort.

The peace program of the Revolutionary Defensists was a shambles. Thus by default the Bolsheviks were in a position to attract the support of the millions of Russians who desired peace above all else. Only some crisis was needed to crystallize this incipient support. It was not long in coming.

FINAL EFFORTS TOWARD PEACE

The political situation in Russia was abruptly altered in the last days of August by an attempted coup by General Kornilov, the supreme commander of the Russian army. The Kornilov affair discredited the Kerensky government and Kerensky personally among broad segments of political opinion, completed the destruction of the army, further undermined Russia's international standing, created havoc with the unity of the Menshevik–Socialist Revolutionary bloc, and brought a dramatic resurgence of Bolshevik popularity, which soon gave the Bolsheviks control not only of the Petrograd Soviet but also of the Moscow Soviet and others. At the same time, by creating such political chaos, the attempted coup stimulated new interest in peace efforts, driving home to many Russians the urgency of peace.

The Kornilov affair itself is a complex and confused story; a clear and detailed account of it is outside the scope of our study.[1] General Kornilov had been appointed supreme commander by Kerensky after the July uprising, to the cheers of the political right, which hailed him as a leader who would revitalize the country and restore public order. Differences soon developed between Kerensky and Kornilov over a number of issues, especially the extent of Kornilov's authority and the amount of counterrevolution needed to stabilize the country. After a period of confused maneuvering on the part of both men, Kornilov led troops against the capital on August 26. The ill-planned move collapsed quickly, but it had many political repercussions, the most important being the rapid resurgence of the Bolsheviks.

The Bolsheviks, weakened and with Lenin in hiding since the July days, rode the wave of popular reaction against Kornilov. They emphasized that they had warned all along of the dangers of a military coup and tarred the Soviet leadership for its association with the government and the army. On September 9 the Tsereteli-led presidium resigned following a no-confidence vote on a Bolshevik resolution. Trotsky replaced Chkheidze as chairman on the 25th, and the Bolsheviks took effective control of the Petrograd Soviet.

The Bolshevik takeover of the Petrograd Soviet forced the Menshevik–Socialist Revolutionary bloc to transfer its base of operations to the Central Executive Committee (TsIK) of the All-Russian Congress of Soviets. This committee, established at the All-Russian Congress in June, had 300 members, 150 elected by the congress on the basis of party affiliation, 100 selected on a territorial basis, and 50 delegated from the Petrograd Soviet. The Tsereteli-led Revolutionary Defensists dominated the committee and ran the day-to-day business of the unwieldy body from its presidium. They had already tended to shift the foundations of their authority from the Petrograd Soviet to the committee, which could claim to represent all of Russia. Now, with the Bolshevik control of the Petrograd Soviet, this became a necessity. Thus the political scene was further clouded in September and October by the existence of three claimants to political authority: the Defensist-dominated Central Executive Committee, the Bolshevik-led Petrograd Soviet, and the Provisional Government. The condition of the government was precarious; it virtually collapsed on September 1, beginning a government crisis that lasted until September 25. The government was in the hands of a Council of Five, headed by Kerensky, while negotiations for its reorganization proceeded. For the first time since the formation of the coalition ministry in May, there was talk of finding a completely new government, even on the part of the Mensheviks and Socialist Revolutionaries.

The frailty of the government and the Bolshevik upsurge led both the Tsereteli group and the government to renew the search for a way to extricate Russia from the war and revive their own rapidly deteriorating political position. The moderate socialists quickly made an attempt to regain their authority and at the same time resolve the political crisis by convoking a Democratic Conference in Petrograd. The invitation was sent in the name of the Central Executive Committee of the All-Russian Congress of Soviets and the Executive Committee of the All-Russian Soviet of Peasants' Deputies.* The purpose, according to Dan, was to create a "democratic" authority, based not on the narrower sense of the word as represented by the soviets but on a wider meaning that would permit the participation of representatives of cooperatives, organs of local self-government, and similar groups. In other words, not only the socialists but also the groups slightly to the right of them politically were to be included; the Cadets did not qualify. The hope was that this body would bolster the Menshevik–Socialist Revolutionary faction against both the far left and the far right. Some of the organizers of the Democratic Conference anticipated that they might be able to create a "democratic" rather than a "coalition" government, and a list of possible ministers was even discussed: Tsereteli was mentioned as Minister-President and Minister of Foreign Affairs; Kerensky was omitted.[2] Another group, headed by Tsereteli, was reluctant to abandon the coalition idea, however, and even saw the possibility of including the Cadets, a move that the majority resolutely opposed on the grounds that the Cadets had supported the Kornilov revolt. The question, then, was how far right to go in search of coalition partners. A "democratic" or "homogeneous" cabinet would allow the government to act with greater vigor and fewer compromises, if it had the will, but the fear of civil war still deterred many, Tsereteli among them, from this course.

The Democratic Conference opened on September 14 and quickly revealed the extent to which the "revolutionary democracy" was in disarray. On the issue of coalition, which had to be

* The All-Russian Soviet of Peasants' Deputies was dominated by Defensist Socialist Revolutionaries and followed Revolutionary Defensist policies. It accepted the lead of the Central Executive Committee on almost all political issues, especially on war and foreign policy. For the text of the invitation, see Browder and Kerensky, III, 1671–72.

settled before anything else could be considered, both the Mensheviks and the Socialist Revolutionaries were badly splintered. Many of them had lost faith in Tsereteli's program, but lacked any other. Some finally abandoned him on the coalition issue— even Dan wavered—and only with great effort was Tsereteli able to get the Menshevik caucus to reaffirm the principle of coalition by a narrow 81–77 vote. However, coalition with the Cadets, the only non-socialist party of significance and hence the only group with whom coalition was meaningful, was rejected, 86 to 51. The Socialist Revolutionaries experienced a similar schism, voting in their caucus 66 to 57 for coalition in principle, but rejecting a broad coalition 28 to 95.[3] Only the Bolsheviks and their followers seemed to be united and to have a clear-cut objective, but that objective was destructive rather than positive. The conference ended in a complete fiasco on September 19, when it followed the pattern of the Menshevik and Socialist Revolutionary caucuses and voted for coalition in principle 766 to 688, then passed two amendments excluding the Cadets and other groups associated with Kornilov. Finally, having reached a point where everyone was dissatisfied, it rejected the amended resolution 813 to 183.[4] Although the questions of war and foreign policy hovered in the background, influencing the arguments on coalition, there was no opportunity to bring them forward for debate.

The presidium of the conference, which was controlled by the Menshevik–Socialist Revolutionary coalition under Tsereteli, salvaged what they could by obtaining permission from the conference to negotiate with Kerensky on the formation of a new cabinet. A new government, the third and final coalition cabinet, was finally put together on September 25. It was weaker than any of its predecessors, lacking the firm support of any major political group, and like the second coalition included a few liberal Cadets and independent bourgeois members. Kerensky remained the major personality of the government, with Tereshchenko still at his side. The only new figure of importance was Gen. A. I. Verkhovskii, who had suddenly risen from

obscurity after the Kornilov affair to take the post of Minister
of War in the Council of Five and in the new coalition. Voitinskii notes that he was the only person who managed to draw a
spark of enthusiasm from the Democratic Conference.[5] Of the
new ministers, none was a political luminary of the first order.
The Bolshevik-controlled Petrograd Soviet passed a resolution
declaring its lack of confidence in the government, and called
for its resignation.[6]

The government, for its part, lost faith in itself, particularly
Tereshchenko. The Kornilov affair appears to have caused Tereshchenko, until then Kerensky's faithful lieutenant, to lose all
confidence in his chief, though there had been signs of increasing disenchantment since the July government crisis. During
the Kornilov affair he had suggested the possibility of dropping
both Kerensky and Kornilov as a way of settling the conflict.[7]
He accepted office in the new government only under protest;
even then he refused to act as vice president of the cabinet and
thus as Kerensky's first assistant, as he had earlier. At one point,
evidently in late September, he even presented his letter of resignation but was persuaded to withdraw it.[8] Rumors of his resignation gained enough currency to be reported in the press as
fact. Meanwhile, his political position had shifted considerably
to the right. According to Buchanan, on more than one occasion
he expressed his conviction of the need for a mild counterrevolution and the exclusion of the Soviets from the government.
He made these views known to the cabinet as well.[9]

It is against the general background of disorder, together with
Tereshchenko's personal disillusionment and shifting political
views, that one must evaluate his actions as Foreign Minister in
September and October. The prospects for fruitful relations
with the Allies in the aftermath of the Kornilov affair were not
good, for the Allies had openly supported Kornilov. The United
States alone seems to have wished Kerensky well, reflecting Wilson's great interest in having the "democratic experiment" in
Russia work. The British and the French, with a tendency to
watch Russian affairs from the narrower viewpoint of military

expediency, seem to have been solely concerned to see that Russia kept warm bodies in the trenches; the United States, which had not suffered the heavy casualties of those countries, was more willing to gamble on democracy. Kornilov had been overwhelmingly favored by the press of all the Allied countries, including the United States. Only the socialist and labor press, along with some of the liberal newspapers, opposed a military takeover and dictatorship in Russia. Given this support of Kornilov, strained Russo-Allied relations were only to be expected.

Disregarding Russian sensibilities, the Allies decided to push ahead with a joint representation to the Russian government. Planned before the Kornilov putsch, the joint effort was designed to stiffen the Russian government's attitude on the war.* Soon after the Kornilov affair ended, the British, French, Italian, and American ambassadors agreed to pursue the idea of sending a joint note about the domestic and military situation in the country,[10] and sent a draft to their governments for approval. The British, French, and Italian governments approved the draft; the United States did not reply. Nevertheless, the American ambassador, David Francis, continued to associate himself with the project.[11] According to Noulens, Tereshchenko shared the sentiments of the projected note and hoped that it would prompt Kerensky to act more decisively.[12] If Noulens is to be believed (he is not always an accurate source), Tereshchenko was most certainly acting on his own and not as a government spokesman. In any case, the statement is not completely out of line with those Tereshchenko was making to Buchanan about the need for a mild counterrevolution.[13] Tereshchenko seems to have been indulging in a little Machiavellism at this time.

* Browder and Kerensky (III, 1625) attribute the initiative in this plan to the French, possibly because Noulens was charged with drawing up the note. In fact, the initiative, both in this instance and in the earlier suggestion (which grew out of the protest suggested at the Allied Conference in London in July–August), came from the British. By this time the British and French had reversed their earlier positions, and the British were the more aggressive of the two in their demands on the Russian government for "order."

The ambassadors waited until Kerensky had completed his efforts to form the new government and then made their representation to Tereshchenko and Kerensky. Francis, who had not received approval from Washington, did not participate. Buchanan read the note on behalf of his colleagues. Referring first to the recent crises and then to the need to defeat Germany, the note continued:

Recent events have thrown doubts on Russia's power of resistance and on the possibility of continuing the struggle. The Allied Governments might soon find themselves confronted by a trend of opinion which would put on trial their responsibility concerning the utility of the considerable sacrifices in arms, munitions, material of every kind accorded without counting to Russia while they would be reproached with not having reserved them for the western front where the wish to conquer appears without faltering.

To restore confidence to this opinion and to give to the Allied Governments the power of reassuring it, it behooves the Russian Government to show by acts its resolve to employ all proper means to revive discipline and true military spirit among the fighting troops, at the same time that it will insure the operation of the public services and the reestablishment of order at the front as at the rear.[14]

According to Noulens, Buchanan read the note in a harsh voice that made the "rather harmless complaints" seem like peremptory injunctions and changed the spirit of the text.[15] Whatever Buchanan's inflections, this was a strong statement for diplomatic envoys to make to an allied country and hardly "harmless complaints." Noulens was more accurate when he also called the statements in the note "truths a little rude."[16] Not unnaturally, the exhausted and high-strung Kerensky was insulted.

Kerensky replied in angry Russian, Tereshchenko translating. He would, he said, try to prevent a "false interpretation" being made of this note by others. After reminding the ambassadors of the sacrifices Russia had made in the war and of the Allies' delays in supplying materials to the Russian army after the revolution, he dismissed them abruptly, declaring that Russia was still a great power.[17] He then rushed to the American embassy to thank Francis for not participating in the démarche, little suspecting why he had not.[18]

Tereshchenko immediately sent a series of three telegrams to the Russian representatives in Rome, London, and Paris. In the first two he gave an account of the ambassadors' presentation and Kerensky's answer, in the third, the Russian government's reaction. The last telegram instructed the Russian representatives to inform their respective Foreign Ministers that "the collective declaration of the three Ambassadors has made a painful impression on us, on account of both its substance and the manner in which it was done." They were also to request that the note not be made public because of the resentment it would cause in Russia.[19]

The Allies immediately realized that the note had been ill-timed, and told the Russian representatives that the declaration had been made with the best of intentions and without any desire to interfere in Russian affairs. Nevertheless, they did not retract the sentiments of the declaration; moreover, they made it clear that they still felt the Russian government should take energetic action against the leftists. All the governments concerned were more than happy not to have the incident publicized and agreed to keep the démarche secret.[20]

This incident did much to accentuate the tension between Russia and the Allies, which became stronger than ever in September and October. An incident related by Noulens illustrates the degree of sensitivity existing between them. In October King George received Gen. V. I. Gurko, who had gone to England after the Provisional Government had relieved him of his post on the grounds that he was politically unreliable. His reception in England was at least in bad taste, if not an intentional slap at the Provisional Government. Kerensky was incensed and told Buchanan that he planned to write a letter of sympathy to the Sinn Féiners.[21] (He did not do so.) Kerensky's bitterness over the actions of the Allies after the Kornilov affair continued long after his fall. Much later he wrote that the course he followed after the Allied démarche had been a mistake: Russia should have taken advantage of the actions of the Allies to withdraw from the alliance and conduct the war as a separate power, defending its own borders![22]

Despite the unhappy state of the relations between Russia and the Allies, the Provisional Government stayed with the alliance and the Allies stayed with Russia. Perhaps nothing more clearly illustrates the fact that both sides were caught in a situation from which they could not escape than the continued futility of the efforts to reach some sort of separate peace with one or more of their opponents in late 1917. Like the earlier attempts, these too foundered on the rocks of wartime animosities and postwar aspirations. Neither the Allies nor the Central Powers felt they could give up their plans for annexations and indemnities after so much effort and suffering. Of all the major powers, only Russia and Austria-Hungary were willing to conclude a peace without annexations or indemnities, in effect accepting the *status quo ante,* but they were the two countries least capable of forcing their partners into a general negotiated peace, and neither was able to find an acceptable way to a separate peace.

The peace effort continued, however, and it constitutes an important part of the later history of the Provisional Government's foreign policy. A number of negligible peace feelers were directed toward Russia by Germany; they came to nothing. However, a more important peace proposal came from Pope Benedict XV on July 19/August 1. The Pope had previously consulted Berlin and Vienna, feeling out their receptivity to a peace proposal emanating from the Vatican. Having received a favorable reply, he then issued a note to the belligerent powers proposing peace on the basis of a restoration of occupied territory and no indemnities.[23] His note mentioned Belgium and Poland specifically but made no reference to Russia, nor was Russia among the recipients of the note.

The Pope's note thoroughly alarmed the Russian government. The Russians knew that the Western Allies had been negotiating with Austria in an attempt to detach her from Germany, but they did not know much more than that.[24] At the same time they also were aware of the close relations between the Vatican and Vienna and of the sentiment in both places that peace must come soon if the Hapsburg monarchy was to survive. Under the circumstances, the Russian government was extremely fearful that the Pope's proposal was an attempt to negotiate a peace between the Western Allies and the Central Powers at the expense of Russia, in order to save the Austrian throne. Kerensky so stated publicly in a speech to the Moscow Conference on August 12.[25]

Tereshchenko immediately contacted the Allies about the Pope's note, expressing his disapproval in strong terms. He realized, however, that for reasons of public opinion any peace proposal must be given consideration, and so he also stressed that the Allies' reply to the Pope's note should be reasonable.[26] In fact, the reaction of the Allied countries had been almost uniformly unfavorable to the Pope's proposal, and after consultation they decided that none of the European Allies would answer the note. The responsibility for the response fell to the United States.[27] The Russian ambassador in Washington therefore hastened to talk with the American officials. On August 6/19 Bakhmetev informed the influential Colonel House that he was disturbed by the Pope's overture and wondered what Wilson's reply would be. He hoped, he said, that Wilson would respond with a statement that the Allies would treat with the German people whenever they were in a position to select their own representatives.[28] Such a statement would effectively counter the Pope's note without seeming to refuse to consider his mediation; moreover, it would have democratic overtones that would be pleasing to Russian opinion. American thinking on the matter was similar, and on August 14/27 the United States answered the Pope's note, rejecting his proposal as unacceptable.[29]

The Germans and Austrians kept the issue alive, however, responding with favorable but vague phrases that left the door open for further action either by the Pope or by the Allies.[30] The German reply aroused the Russian press. *Izvestiia* saw in the Papal note and the German answer an attempt to arrange a peace between the Western Allies and Germany at the expense of Russia. Witness, said *Izvestiia,* the recent rumors that Germany was relinquishing her claims in Belgium but increasing her ambitions in the Baltic and the East. At the same time *Izvestiia* was furious at a statement in the German Social Democratic paper to the effect that the German socialists desired peace, and that it made no difference whether it came through Rome or Stockholm. On the contrary, insisted *Izvestiia,* there was all the difference in the world between a peace negotiated by socialists and one sponsored by the Pope and negotiated between "imperialist governments."[31] A few days later, *Izvestiia* again commented on the continuing efforts of the Pope to mediate a peace: it was clearer than ever that an effort was being made for peace in the West at the expense of Russia.[32] This suspicion was not confined to the socialist press. The liberal *Russkiia Vedomosti* read the same meaning into the Pope's note and the German response. It noted that the Allies had rejected all previous peace moves of the sort, but warned that they might not continue to do so unless Russia resumed active military participation in the war. There was no assurance that the Allies would continue to fight for Russia without Russian aid.[33]

Tereshchenko attacked the German and Austrian replies to the Pope as sheer hypocrisy; it was clear that Germany intended to enter peace negotiations only on the basis of the war map.[34] He tried to play down the fear of a separate peace at Russia's expense, although he, too, must have been uneasy about the question. On September 11, before the German reply to the Pope was known, he issued a denial of the truth of rumors appearing in the papers concerning various peace negotiations.[35] Still, the rumors continued, to the point where the French, British, and Italian ambassadors found it necessary to issue a joint statement on September 20 asserting that talk of a peace by the Allies at Russia's expense was entirely unfounded, and that their governments would never adopt such a policy.[36]

Allied and governmental disclaimers did not entirely dispel

the Russian fears, however, and the story continued to circulate. It was frequently linked to another rumor: Japanese intervention in Russia. Such a possibility was discussed in Allied government circles,[37] though how seriously is problematical. Items had occasionally appeared in the press since summer about an agreement between the Japanese and the Western Allies whereby Japan would intervene in Russia and send troops to the Russo-German front in case of a Russian defection. Despite disclaimers from all the governments concerned, and even in the face of the enormous logistics problems that would confront Japan, with an army 7,000 miles deep in hostile country and only one railroad, the rumor did not die. It was fed by fears about the evident Japanese ambitions in Siberia and by memories of the war of 1904–5. Allied approval was suggested by discussions in the Allied press, including that of Japan, of a Japanese occupation of Siberia, with Russian permission, for the purpose of freeing Russian troops for the front.[38]

Despite a general distrust of the Pope's peace effort, there were Russians who were willing to interpret the German answer to the Pope and other peace rumors differently—as an opportunity to move closer to an end to the war. Baron Boris Nolde, who had been one of Miliukov's assistants at the Foreign Ministry, wrote two articles on the significance of the German reply to the Pope's note. In his view, the widespread discussion of peace and peace terms in Germany in the past months made it obvious that the militarist party had slipped, and that groups more responsive to a moderate and negotiated peace were in the ascendancy. In one article he stated that he declined to draw "practical deductions" from this observation, but desired merely to point out the real situation in Germany. In the other, he admitted that the German reply did not contain the conditions needed to bring the war to an end, but again he emphasized his desire to point out the recent developments in Germany.[39] Despite Nolde's disclaimers, the inference to be drawn from his two articles was obvious: Russia should explore the possibility of a peace with Germany that would permit her to withdraw from the war with her status as a great power reasonably intact.

Nolde's was not a lone voice. He represented a large group of moderates and conservatives in and out of the Cadet Party who, after the Kornilov affair and the resurgence of the Bolsheviks, had concluded that it was necessary to get out of the war in order to concentrate on restoring order in the country. These men were not necessarily reactionaries or monarchists; they had simply appraised the situation and reached the conclusion that Russia's best interests, and their own as well, no longer lay in waging war until victory but in immediate peace and some form of counterrevolution. At meetings of the Cadet Central Committee in the last part of September, Nolde tried to get the party to abandon its "war until victory" stand and to work for a general negotiated peace without victors, although he opposed a separate peace. He was supported in this by M. S. Adzhemov, M. M. Vinaver, Vladimir Nabokov, and A. A. Dobrovolskii, an important bloc on the Cadet Central Committee. Miliukov, however, opposed them, arguing that Russia could still achieve her original war aims. Gen. M. V. Alekseev, who had joined the Cadet Party, lent his military authority to Miliukov's position (although he no longer held a responsible military position, having refused to serve under the current Kerensky regime). Since Miliukov had to leave Petrograd, a decision on the question was deferred until October, when he was to return.[40]

The scheduled meetings did not take place. However, the issue was again debated during the last days of September at a gathering of moderates and conservatives held at the home of a prominent Cadet, Prince G. P. Trubetskoi. Miliukov was not there, but Tereshchenko, Nolde, Vladimir Nabokov, Rodzianko, A. A. Neratov (permanent undersecretary at the Foreign Ministry), V. A. Maklakov (ambassador-designate to Paris, a Cadet), A. I. Konovalov and S. N. Tretiakov (cabinet members), and others were present. The question discussed was whether the current situation, especially the military situation, made serious consideration of peace moves necessary. Nolde again argued that conditions in Russia made peace imperative. Nabokov and Konovalov supported him, as did Maklakov to some extent; Rodzianko and others sharply disagreed.[41] At the beginning of October, then, the ranks of the Cadet Party, and of the liberals and conservatives who gathered around it, were split on the issue of peace. However, Nolde's position remained a minority opinion, as did his evaluation of the Pope's note and the German reply. The attempt to move the Cadet Party and other leading liberal and conservative politicians toward a peace policy failed. Unfortunately, the sources do not indicate what, if anything, Tereshchenko said, or for that matter whether he was a participant in the discussions or simply an observer.

The question of peace would not be stilled, however, and in mid-October, on the eve of the collapse of the Provisional Government, it again came to the fore as a major issue. One reason for its reemergence, apart from the growing realization of the need for peace in both socialist and non-socialist circles, was the approach of another interallied conference, the first to be attended by authoritative Russian representatives who could bring forward war aims and peace as topics for discussion. Russia had not been able to participate in the Allied conferences during the spring and summer; nor had she been able to gain acceptance for her proposal that either revision of war aims be put on the agenda of one of these conferences or a special conference for that purpose be convoked. The conference in London in July–August had decided to hold monthly meetings of the major Allied powers, scheduling the next for September 2/15.[42] This meeting, which was to be attended by Russian cabinet members led by Tereshchenko, had been postponed until late September. Now Tereshchenko asked Buchanan to have the meeting again postponed for a short time. He also requested that it be held in London instead of Paris as planned, since he hoped by that time to have an ambassador there, possibly Prince

Lvov. Buchanan warned Tereshchenko that there would be a frank discussion at the conference of the role Russia would be expected to play in the alliance and of the aid the Allies could be expected to give her. Tereshchenko agreed that such an exchange was needed, and expressed the hope that American delegates would be present.[43] Throughout 1917 the Russians, and Tereshchenko especially, harbored the mistaken view that since Wilson had earlier championed a negotiated peace, and since the United States was less imperialist than the other Allies, the Americans would support the Russian position.

The Kornilov affair upset the schedule for the conference, and it was again postponed, this time until October 21/November 3. Meanwhile, the Russian government continued to make plans for it. In a declaration issued on September 25, the third coalition government took note of Russia's need for peace, and promised to continue its efforts in that direction.

The Provisional Government, working in full agreement with the Allies, will, in the near future, take part in the interallied conference. At this gathering the Government will have among its plenipotentiaries someone who has the special confidence of the democratic organizations.

At this conference, where general war questions common to all the Allies will be decided, our delegates will also strive to come to an understanding with the Allies on the basic principles laid down by the Russian revolution.[44]

The government had difficulty selecting a delegation prestigious enough to give weight to its proposals. General Alekseev was the first choice for military representative, since he was the most authoritative Russian military man available. However, at a meeting at Stavka on September 28, he refused to take part in the conference, asserting that he considered the situation hopeless and would not try to convince the Allies otherwise.[45]

An even greater problem was the selection of someone with "the special confidence of the democratic organizations," i.e., a representative of the socialists, probably from the Central Executive Committee of the All-Russian Congress of Soviets, where the Tsereteli group still held sway. According to Miliukov, this phrase had been carefully worked out as a way to make the Soviet representative a member of the government's delegation and under the government's control. Moreover, he says, in the negotiations to form the cabinet, the Cadets had insisted that this representative was to be named by the government.[46] The socialists either misinterpreted the Cadet demand or else chose to ignore it. On October 7 the Central Executive Committee appointed Skobelev as its representative. The lengthy set of instructions he received reflected the pressure from the left and the growing disarray of the Menshevik–Socialist Revolutionary bloc. They were a potpourri of socialist ideals ranging from disarmament to freedom of the seas (including the neutralization of the Suez and Panama canals), from various territorial settlements to the League of Nations. They also included demands that all obstacles placed in the way of the Stockholm Conference be removed, and that all foreign affairs be democratized. Under the heading "The Way to Peace," the instructions insisted on a general peace congress.[47]

The unrealistic nature of this document is readily apparent. Such far-reaching and selfless demands were far beyond anything any of the warring powers was willing to accept, Russia probably included. The Allies immediately announced their complete rejection of both the instructions of the Central Executive Committee and its delegate. Jules Cambon, of the French Foreign Ministry, announced on October 18/31 that "the Allied governments will absolutely refuse to consent to M. Skobeleff taking part in the deliberations."[48] A similar statement was issued by the British Foreign Office: Skobelev would not be admitted to the conference; only the representatives of the Russian government would be allowed to participate.[49] As if this were not rebuff enough, the French and British emphasized that the subject of the conference would be the energetic prosecution of the war, not war aims and peace.[50]

Despite the Allied reaction, the question of foreign policy, and of the Allied conference in particular, was the topic of heavy debate in the Council of the Republic, or Preparliament, which opened on October 7, the same day the Skobelev instructions were announced. The council, which grew out of the Democratic Conference, represented an attempt by the Provisional Government and the moderate political groups in Russia to provide some sort of foundation for the government, although the government was not responsible to it. The hope was that the council would provide a forum for official policies and bolster the government's sagging prestige. Many hoped also, the Mensheviks and the Socialist Revolutionaries especially, that it would be able to counter the growing Bolshevik strength, which the Democratic Conference had failed to do. The council had only limited functions. It could address questions to the government and discuss important problems, but it had no legislative power; it was purely consultative. In composition it was weighted in favor of the "democratic organizations" (socialist parties and trade unions), which had 367 seats; the "property-owning groups" had 156 and the nationalities (mostly socialists) 27. The strength of the "democratic" group was mostly on paper, however, for included in it were such disparate elements as the Bolsheviks and Plekhanov's intensely pro-war *Edinstvo* group.[51] Fears about the attitude and activities of the Bolsheviks in the council were resolved the first day, when Trotsky violently denounced the "council of counterrevolutionary connivance" and the "government of betrayal of the people," and led the Bolsheviks out of the hall.[52] After this sensational beginning, the council busied itself with long and fruitless debates.

Tereshchenko made a lengthy report at a closed session of the Foreign Affairs Committee of the council, in which he evaluated the military-political situation of Russia and the other powers. For the first time during his tenure of office, he formally outlined with reasonable clarity and precision his foreign policy objectives. As minimum conditions for peace he listed: 1) access to the Baltic Sea and an absolute guarantee that no autonomous buffer states, which might gravitate toward Germany, would be created along the Baltic; 2) access to the Mediterranean, which might be achieved by a number of methods (he did not specify his own preference); and 3) economic independence, which could be best served by close economic ties with the Allied countries, and which could not be maintained if Germany were victorious. Tereshchenko also emphasized that the forthcoming interallied conference would be concerned primarily with questions of defense and prosecution of the war and only tangentially with revision of the treaties. It would not, he said, be a direct preparation for peace.[53] He had traveled a long distance since May!

And yet, it was not so much Tereshchenko's position that had changed as his emphasis. This is clear from a long exchange he had with Miliukov following his address. In the course of the discussion, he stated that Russia had not put these conditions before the Allies, because she did not wish to relinquish her claims without knowing whether the Allies would follow suit. The question of revision of the treaties, he declared, must be considered from the point of view of expediency as well as principle. In his opinion, he said, the agreements on the partition of Turkey were a liability, since the division of Asia Minor between the Allied powers held dangers for Russia in the event of an incomplete solution of the Straits problem.[54] In other words, Tereshchenko was unwilling to give up control of the Straits if any major power—France, Britain, or Italy—were to be ensconced in Asia Minor; until they renounced their annexations there, Russia could not relinquish her claims to the Straits. Here, Tereshchenko became the traditional Russian statesman, fearful of the establishment of a strong European power in Asia Minor. The position he took was not really different from his earlier stand, except in its forthrightness.

Two other statements Tereshchenko made help to clarify his foreign policy as well as confirm the trend of his thought. At one point in the exchange with Miliukov, he made it clear that he felt Russia and the Allies would have to work out a negotiated peace with Germany, not for the sake of principle but because the military situation offered little prospect of total victory for either side.[55] Later, referring to the possible loss of the Baltic region through the application of the principle of self-determination, he asserted that "in general, the formula for the self-determination of nations is not a single one, and it allows for very different applications in practice."[56] Thus, though Tereshchenko continued to recognize the need for peace, he sought it through traditional diplomatic channels, accepting the consequence of continuing the war, for a while at least, as a faithful member of the alliance. The stance of the exponent of new methods in foreign policy was gone. Even more important, the emphasis on a peace in the near future was gone—a most significant shift of emphasis indeed.

Foreign affairs was taken up by the council again, this time on October 16 before a general session. Tereshchenko made a formal appearance before a public body for the first time in his career as Foreign Minister. In his speech, he stressed that Russia's vital interests, both political and economic, required her to remain an active partner in the alliance, and reiterated the minimum foreign policy program he had outlined at the committee meeting. The most important part of his speech, however, concerned the interallied conference and Skobelev's attendance: at the Allied conference, as at the peace conference, Russia would have a single delegation and would speak with a single unified voice. The delegates who had the "trust of the democracy" would be members of the government's delegation and subordinate to him, as head of the delegation, he said firmly.[57] The next day he again attacked the mandate of Skobelev before the Foreign Affairs Committee of the council and insisted anew on a unified delegation at the conference.[58]

Tereshchenko's change of emphasis, the shift from seeking an immediate peace to carrying on the war in union with the Allies as a matter of necessity rather than choice, was challenged in the cabinet by a simultaneous shift in the other direction by the Minister of War, General Verkhovskii. Verkhovskii, who had entered the government in the wake of the Kornilov affair, had aroused considerable attention as a young (34), vigorous, reform-minded, if somewhat impetuous and politically unsophisticated, soldier. As military commissar, Voitinskii had opportunity and reason to observe the young general closely, and described him as "politically ignorant but sensible and devoid of the caste prejudices of military technicians."[59] Though of aristocratic background, Verkhovskii had something of a democratic touch; apparently he had been in trouble as a young officer for trying to prevent soldiers from firing on a crowd during a civil disturbance. A colonel at the outbreak of the revolution, he rose rapidly during the search for "democratic officers." He evidently did not agree with some of his cabinet colleagues on various policies, notably when he sought to strengthen the army by drastically cutting its size to make it better organized and disciplined, and he had clashed with Tereshchenko in particular.[60] Verkhovskii made numerous visits to meetings of political parties and met with various political leaders frequently, trying to obtain support for his policies; his cabinet colleagues must surely have disapproved.*

Verkhovskii's worry about the unwillingness of the soldiers to fight and the military difficulties arising from the political and economic disorder in the country led him to conclude that peace was essential. He later claimed the event that finally brought him to this conclusion was General Alekseev's refusal to go to the Allied conference as Russia's military representative: on September 23, on the way back to Petrograd from the meeting with Alekseev, he had decided that an immediate peace was necessary.[61] What actions he may have taken immediately after this are not known, but on October 20 he asked to meet privately with some leading members of the Cadet Party. At the meeting he insisted on the need to enter into immediate peace negotiations, citing the extreme perilousness of Russia's military and supply condition. It was impossible to continue to fight, he concluded; a way out of the war must be found before

---

* Chernov (Ts. k-t P. S. R., pp. 14–15) describes Verkhovskii's appearance at a meeting of the Socialist Revolutionaries' Central Committee on September 11. Among the other political groups he met with were the Cadets and the Central Executive Committee. See Slavin, pp. 12–17.

disaster overtook the country. He then asked if he could count on the support of the Cadets. Verkhovskii had badly mistaken his audience, however, evidently assuming that Nolde's views were widely held in the party,* and he was severely rebuked.[62] Miliukov still dominated the party and refused to countenance the idea of peace short of full victory. According to Miliukov, Verkhovskii also approached the leaders of other factions in the Council of the Republic with the same arguments.[63]

Verkhovskii was not to be denied, however. Later the same day he repeated his plea for an immediate peace at a closed joint session of the council's committees on Foreign Affairs and Defense. He made a lengthy survey of the unsatisfactory conditions in the army, summarizing them as follows:

1) the reduction of the army to a desirable size cannot be carried out for strategical reasons; 2) under these conditions the army cannot be fed; 3) similarly, it cannot be properly clothed . . . ; 4) there is no one to take command; 5) bolshevism is continuing to corrupt our combatant forces.[64]

He argued that there was only one conclusion to be drawn from these facts: Russia could no longer fight and must therefore initiate peace negotiations. To do so would cut the ground from under the "noxious" elements in the country, and anarchy could then be suppressed by means of the more reliable units of the army. The Allies could be pressured into agreeing to peace, he believed, by two arguments: "First, in spite of our weakness, we are holding 130 enemy divisions on our front, and second, our indebtedness to the Allies, which has reached the sum of 20 billion [rubles]."[65] Verkhovskii's reasoning on the salutary effects of peace inside Russia may have been sound, but like everyone else he was unable to find any real lever to force the Allies into a negotiated peace (assuming that Germany was willing). The Allies had decided as early as July that they could cope with the defection of Russia and the release of the German troops in the east, if necessary, and the financial argument was hardly strong enough to force the Allies to make peace.

---

* It is possible the Nolde led him into this meeting as part of his own campaign to swing the Cadets to a peace stance.

Verkhovskii was challenged by Tereshchenko and others. Several charged that he was fulfilling German war aims. He replied that it was time to turn from eloquent phrases to sober reality: "We must decide what we can afford and what we cannot afford. If we do not have the means for a better peace, we must conclude the kind of peace that is now possible." However, when asked what the Russian response should be if the Allies rejected his proposal for peace, he replied: "in that case, being bound by certain commitments, we would have to submit to fate, i.e., go through such trials as a Bolshevik rising, . . . anarchy, and all the repercussions that follow it."[66] Verkhovskii thus drew back from the horror of a separate peace, as had Tsereteli and Tereshchenko before him, and again the result was political sterility. Studying this repeated reluctance to risk everything on a move that was not only a radical break with past policy but a break whose repercussions could not be foreseen, one is tempted to suggest that perhaps the successor Bolshevik government is to be more distinguished from its predecessors by its willingness to cut through this and other thorny problems, without regard for perils such as civil war or German domination, than by ideological or organizational differences; the difference may have been more a matter of temperament than doctrine.

A more skilled politician than Verkhovskii would have organized a show of support for his declaration in advance, which Voitinskii claims he might well have been able to do among the representatives of army committees present, as well as among some of the political figures, Menshevik, Socialist Revolutionary, and Cadet. He did not, however; instead he made his declaration without warning, and in an almost flippant and theatrical manner, evidently expecting the shock of his speech to change Russian foreign policy in a moment.[67] It was a romantic—and unsuccessful—idea. Verkhovskii's resignation was a foregone conclusion. Tereshchenko went directly to Kerensky and demanded his removal. The request granted, he returned to the hall of the council quite pleased with his victory over his opponent.[68] Kerensky asked Verkhovskii to leave Petrograd immediately,[69] and the papers announced that the general had gone to Finland for a two-week leave.[70] An attempt was made to keep the affair quiet, but one Petrograd newspaper, *Obshchee Delo*, revealed the substance of Verkhovskii's speech before the committees, wrongly adding that he had called for a separate peace; it was promptly closed down. Verkhovskii issued a statement denying the *Obshchee Delo* report, as did Skobelev and Znamenskii, the chairmen of the two committees.[71] No one bothered to point out, however, that the report was essentially accurate, the part about a separate peace excepted.

By this time the debates on war and peace, and on the interallied conference and revision of war aims, were taking on a more frantic tone, as talk of a Bolshevik coup became more frequent. In retrospect these discussions have an unreal air, but that results from a tendency to assess everything in light of the imminent Bolshevik takeover. In the perspective of the time, a Bolshevik seizure of power was only a possibility (though becoming more real daily), a possibility, moreover, that made the issue of peace the more urgent, for only vigorous action in this area gave much hope of reversing the Bolshevik rise.

The government, however, did nothing. When its own Minister of War stated bluntly that the army could no longer be maintained and peace was urgent, it could think of nothing better to do than dismiss him and hush up the scandal. Hypnotized by the enormity of the problems facing it, the government followed a course of politics as usual. The response of the moderate socialists in the Central Executive Committee was hardly more effective in the face of the imminent threat. They had not developed a new foreign policy program after Stockholm and clung vainly to the shreds of that program. Still, they recognized the need for a final, desperate effort. Dan, who led the weakened forces of Revolutionary Defensism in the absence of Tsereteli (who had taken ill and left the capital), made a belated effort to prod the government. In speeches on October 24 in the Council of the Republic and the Central Executive Committee, he argued that, though the main danger lay in the counterrevolutionary thrust that would follow a Bolshevik attempt to seize power, the government must act decisively to defuse the Bolshevik threat. Specifically, it must take immediate steps to begin peace negotiations and domestic reforms, especially land distribution, and must post notices throughout Petrograd that very night announcing its intentions. Only this, he argued, might dissuade the garrison troops from following the Bolsheviks in attempting a coup. Dan and Gots called on Kerensky the same day to urge him to act along this line, but were rebuffed.[72]

As for the liberal and conservative opponents of Bolshevism, they literally fiddled while the Russia they believed in went up in smoke. After a depressing session of the Council of the Republic the evening before the Bolshevik coup, a small group gathered at the house of A. I. Kaminka, a prominent Cadet. They found there was little to say, and the atmosphere was heavy with gloom and apprehension. To ease the tension, they decided to have music, and someone jokingly proposed that Miliukov be called to come over and play his violin. Miliukov responded with alacrity, as if awaiting the invitation, and was soon attacking a Beethoven sonata.[73]

WAR AND REVOLUTION: SOME CONCLUSIONS

The collapse of the Tsarist government threw Russia into a new "Time of Troubles," such as it had undergone three centuries earlier. The first raised the Romanovs to the throne; the second saw their demise and the ascendancy of the Bolsheviks. In the period of the Provisional Government, February to October 1917, the opening act of this new time of troubles, the men of the February revolution tried to establish a stable, progressive regime in Russia. Most certainly they were aware of the danger of a complete collapse and political chaos. Ironically, their fear of civil turmoil was a major factor in their failure, for it constantly paralyzed their will to decisive action. Whenever the demand for vigorous, even radical, action was raised, both the Provisional Government and the Soviet leaders held back, fearing that civil war and even foreign intervention would ensue if they proceeded too far too fast. They had the memory not only of their own time of troubles but of the French Revolution, the nineteenth-century European revolutions, and more recently their own revolution of 1905 to remind them of this danger. If nothing else, the Russian intelligentsia was familiar with historical precedent.[1] When one looks back on the history of 1918–21, who is to say their caution was ill-founded?

Of all the issues that shaped 1917, none was more pressing or more paralyzing than the problem of war and peace. It was the overwhelming desire for peace that opened the way for the more radical development of the revolution, for the so-called "deepening of the revolution." This desire was exploited first by the Mensheviks and the Socialist Revolutionaries in their struggle with Miliukov, and then by the Bolsheviks against the Mensheviks–Socialist Revolutionaries. The turmoil over the war and peace question hindered attempts to consolidate and order the gains already achieved by the revolution, and stymied efforts to carry out reforms and deal with problems in other areas. It was generally assumed, and possibly correctly so, that until peace was attained most of the other problems could not be settled. How to distribute the land while almost ten million peasants were in the army? How to deal with economic chaos while its main cause, the war, continued? How to deal intelligently and dispassionately with the national minorities while the frontiers of the country were invaded and its very survival threatened?

Whoever the leaders, then, the first priority had to be to find a way out of the war. The most direct means, a separate peace with Germany and Austria, was rejected out of hand by every political group; even the Bolsheviks heatedly denied that their demands for an immediate end to the war meant a separate peace. It was a general article of faith that Russia had more in common with the Western democracies than with Germany; that the best possibility for the development of a democratic society, socialist or other, lay in a world dominated by the Western powers rather than by militarist Germany; that a separate peace or truce, even on favorable terms, would allow Germany to win the war in the west; and that a German victory would make Russia politically and economically dependent on Germany, and possibly even lead to a restoration of the monarchy. Although Russia might have obtained better peace terms in the spring of 1917 than in 1918—and that is by no means certain, given German hopes for the success of submarine warfare—the terms of Brest–Litovsk must make the historian hesitate to dismiss Russian fears of the nature of a separate peace as groundless. The final dilemma of the moderates, a separate peace or continued war, was awesome in its magnitude and paralyzing in its probable consequences. Even the Bolsheviks faltered before it. Only desperation, together with the iron will and fanatic self-confidence of Lenin, drove them to accept a separate peace, and only the victory of the Allies rescued them from the fate the moderates had predicted. In retrospect we know that circumstances beyond Russia's control allowed her to survive the draconian terms of Brest–Litovsk, but the men of 1917 could not anticipate this in contemplating peace terms. From that vantage point, one could as logically choose the other alternative, in the hope that the extremists could be fended off somehow, and Russia would be able to stagger on until the war ended in an Allied victory. It was even possible to believe, as Miliukov told Nabokov on one occasion, that perhaps the war held things together, and that without it everything would quickly fall apart.[2] As faulty, even ridiculous, as such reasoning seems now, it was not as illogical from the perspective of the times as it is with our knowledge of what followed.

It is small wonder, given the unhappy results to be expected from either a separate peace or continued war, that the only viable foreign policy seemed to be to seek a general negotiated peace. The strength of the Revolutionary Defensists led by Tsereteli was that they were the first to elaborate a coherent program designed to obtain a general peace without sacrificing the revolution or the country. It was their good fortune to arrive on the scene at a time when a wave of war-weariness was sweeping Europe and a negotiated peace seemed feasible. Their peace program was all the more attractive because it was a two-pronged effort. On one side it relied on government diplomacy (revolutionized by a stress on publicity and the rejection of secrecy) to prepare the ground for peace by getting the Allies to accept the slogan of "peace without annexations or indemnities, self-determination of peoples." This, it was hoped, would bring peace nearer by showing the Central Powers that negotiation was possible. Then, there was the more revolutionary side, the stress on the role the European proletariat, or democracy, would play. The Revolutionary Defensist program assumed that the governments of the warring countries would accept the Russian peace formula only under pressure from their proletariats. To this end, it was considered necessary to convoke an international conference of socialist and labor parties to work out a coordinated peace campaign. These two policies, the governmental and the socialist, were to be a joint effort and were to reinforce each other.

Both policies failed. They were wrecked first of all by the opposition of the Allies, whose cooperation was essential. The Revolutionary Defensists had a peculiar love-hate attitude toward the Allies. On the one hand, the Allied governments were by definition bourgeois, capitalist, imperialist, and hostile to socialist revolution. On the other, the Soviet leaders as well as the liberals considered Britain and France the most progressive countries of Europe, countries with which cooperation was not only possible but necessary. This ambivalence carried over to the Allied socialist parties. Ideology insisted that the socialists and working class of Europe be antiwar, revolutionary, and united; reality showed them to be divided and in the main nationalistic. The confused and uncertain attitude of the Defensists resulted in both high hopes and political paralysis in the face of anticipated or real opposition. It led to long and fruitless discussion with the Allied socialists and labor groups, whose own attitude toward the Russian revolution and peace program was ambivalent. By first accepting the Soviet program—willingly or reluctantly—and then acquiescing in its destruction by their governments rather than forcing its acceptance, as the Revolutionary Defensists believed they would do, the Allied socialists contributed directly to the collapse of Revolutionary Defensism.

The leaders of the Allied governments, for their part, were determined on a decisive victory, and in this they were supported by the great majority of their constituents. At first they hesitated over how best to deal with the Russian revolution, especially the British, and this encouraged the Revolutionary Defensists. But by midsummer, when the Russian peace offensive was fully launched, the military and political picture had changed in the west; there was increasing evidence that the war could be won, with or without Russia. The entry of the United States into the war, the failure of the German submarine offensive, and the recession of the earlier wave of weariness and defeatism in Europe left the peace movement stranded and the Allied governments and peoples convinced that victory was in sight. The Allied governments therefore blocked the Stockholm Conference by refusing passports to the socialists and at the same time delayed action on the proposals of the Russian government for a revision of the treaties outlining war aims. A policy of procrastination succeeded in warding off a socialist-inspired peace, but at the cost of assisting the rise of Bolshevism.

Even if the Allies had agreed to revise their goals, peace would not necessarily have been a corollary. The Allies had protested over and over again that they fought only for justice and right. A new declaration along that line, even if accompanied by a public renunciation of the secret treaties, would probably not have had much effect, apart from exposing the hypocrisy of their earlier statements. Moreover, Russian peace efforts were directed toward the task of persuading the Allies to accept the idea of a negotiated peace; the Russians never came to grips with the thorny problem of whether Germany, where the military clique around Ludendorff and Hindenburg was in control, was in fact willing to negotiate a peace.

There is also the question of the extent to which the Russian government energetically pushed for a negotiated peace. Although the various coalition governments never reverted entirely to Miliukov's program of victory at any cost, neither were they especially vigorous in their efforts to overcome Allied opposition to a negotiated peace. The first coalition government seemed to make a serious attempt to work out a general peace, though it moved slowly, always waiting for the right opportunity, the favorable conditions that never came. After July and August, however, the government, and especially Tereshchenko, gradually abandoned the idea of a negotiated peace as an immediate objective. Peace was still considered desirable, even necessary, but the realities of international politics made it clear that a negotiated peace was not likely in the fall of 1917. Only in October, in the last days of the Provisional Government, did Tereshchenko return to the policy of peace through revision of war aims. Even then, it appears that he did so more in the hope of strengthening the army than in a belief that a revision would lead to peace.

Finally, the nature of the Soviet leadership and its support must be taken into account. The Tsereteli group had worked out an attractive peace scheme, one that appealed to both the desire for peace and the patriotism of a broad segment of the population, including the Russian soldiers. That program rested, however, on a mistaken evaluation of European socialism. It assumed that European—and especially Allied—socialists would quickly be converted into fervent supporters of a negotiated peace based on the Soviet formula. Even more erroneously, it assumed that they could and would force their respective governments to change their fundamental war and foreign policies. Finally, it also assumed an ability to control the political situation in Russia, a control that was not in fact possible. Even if workable, the Defensists' peace program by its very complexity required a great deal of time and patience. Time and patience their followers would not give them; explanations of the difficulties of reuniting international socialism and of the intricacies of international diplomacy fell on deaf and unsympathetic ears. The Defensist mood of March rapidly evaporated among the troops, especially in Petrograd. The efforts to send troops to the front and the support of the offensive were regarded by the soldiers as a breach of faith; they had been assured that peace was near. Increasingly impatient to end the war so that they could return home and get on with land distribution, the soldiers abandoned the faltering peace efforts of the Mensheviks and the Socialist Revolutionaries, and listened instead to the siren call of the Bolsheviks.

No matter how one sifts the evidence, a general peace appears to have been out of the question in 1917. Interesting as the various peace feelers and negotiations were, one has to be unduly optimistic to see in them any real prospect of a negotiated peace. Most of them were not so much attempts to achieve peace as they were efforts to weaken the opposition by detaching an ally. The war had been too long and too bloody; no statesman could turn to the public and advocate a peace resembling the *status quo ante*, much less give up any territory to the enemy. The efforts of the Russian socialists to bring European public opinion around to the idea of such a peace were unavailing. What French government could have made peace without Alsace-Lorraine; what German government could have given it up? And this was only one disputed area; there were many others on which neither side felt it could yield after so much had been sacrificed. Europe had not yet reached the stage of exhaustion that would make such a peace palatable. In fairness to the men who led the Provisional Government and the Soviet, it must be admitted that they faced an almost impossible task. If their hopes of socialist unity and influence were somewhat utopian and their actions sometimes lethargic, the goal they were working for was in all probability beyond their reach. Both Russia and international socialism were too weak to compel either the Allies or Germany to make a general peace. Having rejected a separate peace, the Russian leaders were forced simply to hang on, to wait either for the war to end or for European peace sentiment to come to the rescue of their program. Russian public opinion, however, was far ahead of that of Europe on the issue of peace and was moving swiftly toward a radical solution of the question. There was no time to wait. The default of the moderates on the promise of peace, though it did not completely guarantee the Bolshevik success, did surrender the initiative to the Bolsheviks on this critical issue and did ensure the moderates' own destruction.

NOTES

Notes

CHAPTER I

1. Shulgin, p. 178, as translated in Golder, *Documents*, p. 267.
2. Sukhanov, *Russian Revolution*, p. 93.
3. There is extensive literature on the first days of the revolution, and no attempt will be made to survey it all here. An important source for the early days is *Izvestiia revoliutsionnoi nedeli: izdanie komiteta petrogradskikh zhurnalistov*, a special newspaper published during the first days of the revolution, when the regular press was closed down. The first issues of the regular papers contain numerous useful articles as well. Particularly valuable memoir accounts by socialists are: Sukhanov, *Zapiski*, Vols. I and II (the abridged English translation, *The Russian Revolution, 1917*, contains most of these volumes); Zenzinov, "Fevralskie dni," XXXV; and Stankevich, pp. 80–91. The best account of events in Duma circles is found in the memoirs of Shulgin, a conservative member. Miliukov, *Istoriia*, Part 1, pp. 40–58, presents a liberal point of view. Peshekhonov's article "Pervyia nedeli" is a generally overlooked but valuable account by a prominent moderate socialist of developments in Petrograd outside the Soviet and Duma centers. A number of valuable documents and excerpts are to be found in Browder and Kerensky, I, 21–152, and II, 846–49. Soviet writing on February has been voluminous but is not particularly valuable. Probably the best is Burdzhalov's detailed study of the February days.
4. Sukhanov, *Russian Revolution*, pp. 116–26. The text of the proclamation is in Browder and Kerensky, I, 135–36.
5. Stankevich, pp. 92–93; Sukhanov, *Russian Revolution*, pp. 8–9, 104–7; Woytinsky, pp. 152–53; *Rabochaia Gazeta*, No. 39, April 25. *Rabochaia Gazeta* was the official Menshevik newspaper.
6. Zenzinov, "Fevralskie dni," XXXV, 225–31; Sukhanov, *Russian Revolution*, pp. 140–43; *Izvestiia*, No. 4, March 3. There were many newspapers titled *Izvestiia*; when used without modifiers it refers to the official organ of the Petrograd Soviet (and later of the Central Executive Committee of the All-Russian Congress of Soviets).

CHAPTER II

1. Cited in Browder and Kerensky, I, 157.

2. Miliukov, "Konstantinopol," which is a collection of articles he wrote just before and in the early weeks of the February Revolution.

3. Miliukov, *Nicholas to Stalin*, p. 106.

4. Nolde, "Nabokov," p. 10.

5. *Rech*, No. 59, March 10. *Rech* was the central organ of the Cadet Party.

6. See *ibid.*, No. 55, March 5, for Miliukov's request that the Foreign Ministry personnel remain on the job. For a good example of socialist criticism of Miliukov's failure to revolutionize the Foreign Ministry personnel, see "The Augean Stables," in *Delo Naroda*, No. 25, April 15. This publication was the central organ of the Socialist Revolutionaries. Insights into the impact of the revolution on Russian embassies can be found in Schatzky, pp. 359–60; and pp. 286–87.

7. For a Russian Foreign Ministry resumé of these agreements, see Browder and Kerensky, II, 1054–57.

8. As quoted in Browder and Kerensky, II, 1042–43. An abbreviated version of the telegram can be found in United States, *Records*, File No. 861.00/287.

9. Adamov, *Konstantinopol*, I, 467–68.

10. *Ibid.*, pp. 470–72.

11. Paléologue, III, 247–48. At this time the Foreign Minister met daily with the major Allied ambassadors.

12. Knox, II, 585.

13. "Iz dnevnika Boldyreva," p. 260.

14. Sukhanov, *Zapiski*, II, 50, 144–49; Pokrovskii and Iakovlev, I (*Protokoly*), 27.

15. *Izvestiia*, No. 16, March 16.

16. Ermanskii, p. 160.

17. Golder, *Documents*, pp. 325–26.

18. *Izvestiia*, No. 18, March 18. For an example of the attempt to gloss over differences, see *Rech*, No. 63, March 15.

19. Even Trotsky, in his description of the Soviet Menshevik–Socialist Revolutionary leaders, acknowledges Tsereteli's leadership; moreover, he lets a ray of respect slip through his invective. See Trotsky, *History*, I, 227–29.

20. See Nikolaevskii, "Tsereteli" (Nos. 730–36, 738-39) for a seven-part study of Tsereteli's life to 1907, written on the occasion of his death.

21. Woytinsky, p. 255.

22. Voitinskii, manuscript, p. 36.

23. Aronson, pp. 25–33.

24. This summary of the ideas of Siberian Zimmerwaldism is drawn from my article "Irakli Tsereteli."

25. Tsereteli, *Vospominaniia*, I, 29–30; Woytinsky, 252–53.

26. Voitinskii, manuscript, pp. 27–28.

27. Tsereteli, *Vospominaniia*, I, 46–47; Sukhanov, *Zapiski*, II, 336–39; Shliapnikov, III, 183–89. The minutes of this meeting, and those of many others, were not preserved. Despite the importance of the meeting, it was not reported in *Izvestiia* or by the press in general. The only two sources of value are the memoirs of the two main antagonists at the meeting, Sukhanov and Tsereteli. Fortunately, they are in essential agreement on what happened. Shliapnikov, who misdates the meeting, adds a little, but he is skimpy on details and makes himself, not Sukhanov, the main opponent of Tsereteli.

28. Tsereteli, *Vospominaniia*, I, 47–53; Sukhanov, *Zapiski*, II, 339–44.

29. Tsereteli, *Vospominaniia*, I, 53–54; Sukhanov, *Zapiski*, II, 344–45.

30. Tsereteli, *Vospominaniia*, I, 55; Sukhanov, *Zapiski*, II, 345–46.

31. Voitinskii, manuscript, pp. 7–9.

32. Stankevich, pp. 78–80. An almost identical evaluation is given, though in more hostile terms, by one of the leftist leaders of the Executive Committee of the Soviet in March. See Steklov, *Vospominaniia*, pp. 79–80.

33. As noted, the only real information on the meetings is provided by Voitinskii. See his manuscript, pp. 59–60. The meetings are briefly discussed in Zenzinov, "Zlodeianie," p. 126. Tsereteli has scattered references in his memoirs, but does not indicate how frequently they were held or how they were conducted. Sukhanov also refers to them in *Zapiski*, but he did not participate and did not quite know what they were or how they operated.

34. Voitinskii, manuscript, pp. 58–59.

CHAPTER III

1. See for example, *Rabochaia Gazeta*, No. 7, March 14; *Delo Naroda*, No. 9, March 27; *Izvestiia*, No. 18, March 18; and Kerensky's press interview printed in the *New York Times*, March 22 (9).

2. *Rech*, No. 70, March 23; reprinted in Browder and Kerensky, II, 1044.

3. *Izvestiia*, No. 26, March 28; *Delo Naroda*, No. 10, March 26; V. Nabokov, pp. 57–58.

4. Sukhanov, *Zapiski*, II, 349–51; Tsereteli, *Vospominaniia*, I, 62–65; Miliukov, *Istoriia*, Part 1, 85; V. Nabokov, p. 58.

5. Tsereteli, *Vospominaniia*, I, 65–68; Sukhanov, *Zapiski*, II, 351–52; V. Nabokov, p. 59; Miliukov, *Vospominaniia*, II, 345.

6. V. Nabokov, p. 59–60.

7. Miliukov, *Istoriia*, Part 1, pp. 86–87; V. Nabokov, pp. 59–60; Tsereteli, *Vospominaniia*, I, pp. 69–72; Sukhanov, *Russian Revolution*, pp. 249–51.

8. Tsereteli, *Vospominaniia*, I, 72; Sukhanov, *Russian Revolution*, pp. 252–53.

9. As translated in Golder, *Documents*, p. 330.

10. *Rabochaia Gazeta*, No. 19, March 28; *Izvestiia*, No. 29, March 31.

11. Pokrovskii and Iakovlev, IV (*Soveshchanie sovetov*), 39–40. This is the stenographic record of the conference.

12. *Ibid.*, pp. 93–96.

13. Browder and Kerensky, II, 1084.

14. *Manchester Guardian*, April 26 (13).

15. See text in Shliapnikov, IV, 324–26.

16. No. 26, April 8.   17. No. 28, April 8.

18. Lenin, XXIV, 21–22.   19. *Pravda*, No. 27, April 8.

20. See the description of their respective reactions in Voitinskii, manuscript, pp. 44–52; Sukhanov, *Zapiski*, III, 7–61; and Ermanskii, p. 155. Sukhanov also vividly describes the hostile reaction of some of the soldiers.

21. Chernov's attacks on Miliukov can be found in various April issues of *Delo Naroda* and are well summarized in Radkey, pp. 157–58.

22. Tsereteli, *Vospominaniia*, I, 83–84.

23. Sukhanov, *Russian Revolution*, p. 310.

24. Sukhanov, *Zapiski*, III, 203–5; Tsereteli, *Vospominaniia*, I, 84–85.

25. Ribot, *Letters*, pp. 209–10; Paléologue, III, 297. The French delegates were Marius Moutet, Marcel Cachin, and Ernest LaFont; the British delegates were Will Thorne, James O'Grady, and William Sanders.

26. Paléologue, III, 300. On the reception of the Allied socialists, see also Sukhanov, *Russian Revolution*, p. 261; Tsereteli, *Vospominaniia*, I, 160–80 *passim*; Shliapnikov, IV, 6–12.

27. Tsereteli, *Vospominaniia*, I, 170–82; Sukhanov, *Zapiski*, III, 184–88.

28. Ribot, *Letters*, p. 211; Drachkovitch, p. 118.

29. Buchanan, II, 119.

30. Miliukov, *Nicholas to Stalin*, p. 105.

31. Kerensky, *Catastrophe*, p. 134.

32. *Rech*, No. 85, April 13; reprinted in Browder and Kerensky, II, 1096.

33. Kerensky, *Catastrophe*, p. 134; V. Nabokov, p. 63; Miliukov, *Istoriia*, Part 1, p. 92. The denial, published in the official government newspaper, *Vestnik Vremennogo Pravitelstvo*, is reprinted in Browder and Kerensky, II, 1097.

34. See, for example, *Delo Naroda*, No. 25, April 5, which declared: "We are for the Provisional Government, but against Miliukov."

35. Tsereteli, *Vospominaniia*, I, 85.

36. Miliukov to Izvolskii, the Russian ambassador to France, April 17, in Adamov, *Konstantinopol*, I, 484; reprinted in Browder and Kerensky, II, 1097.

37. *Ibid.*

38. Kerensky, *Catastrophe*, p. 135; V. Nabokov, p. 63.

39. Text of note is in Browder and Kerensky, II, 1098.

40. Tsereteli, *Vospominaniia*, I, 85–90; Voitinskii, manuscript, pp. 65–66; Sukhanov, *Zapiski*, III, 251–53.

41. *New York Times*, May 5.

42. See "Aprelskie dni 1917" for the report of the commission appointed to investigate the events of the April days. Extensive accounts of the street demonstrations and clashes are to be found in the various newspapers of the time, and also in Miliukov, *Istoriia*, Part 1, pp. 94–99; Voitinskii, manuscript, pp. 66–67; Woytinsky, pp. 270–74; Sukhanov, *Russian Revolution*, pp. 316–20, and *Velikaia, Aprelskii krizis*, pp. 725–801. On the activities of the Bolsheviks during the April crisis, see Rabinowitch, pp. 44–45.

43. Tsereteli, *Vospominaniia*, I, 95–96.

44. Sukhanov, *Zapiski*, III, 266–70; Tsereteli, *Vospominaniia*, I, 101–2; Voitinskii, manuscript, p. 68.

45. Stankevich, p. 115.

46. The course of the session can be pieced together from scattered sources. For accounts by some of the participants, see Tsereteli, *Vospominaniia*, I, 96–103; Stankevich, p. 115; Voitinskii, manuscript, pp. 68–69; Sukhanov, *Zapiski*, III, 285; Chernov, *Great Revolution*, pp. 201–2; Shliapnikov, III, 103–18; and Miliukov, *Istoriia*, Part 1, pp. 95–96. Though the meeting was closed to the press, information was leaked, and reports can be found in *Delo Naroda*, No. 30, April 22; *Rech*, No. 93, April 22; and *Izvestiia*, No. 47, April 22. See also Pokrovskii and Iakovlev, I (*Protokoly*), 118: session of April 21. Kerensky did not attend the meeting.

47. Text is in Browder and Kerensky, II, 1100.

48. *New York Times*, May 8, p. 1.

49. Buchanan, II, 124; Mints, "Pervyi krizis vlast," p. 11.

50. Buchanan, II, 124–25.

51. See, for example, *Izvestiia*, No. 47, April 21; and *Delo Naroda*, No. 30, April 22.

52. Voitinskii (manuscript, p. 77) gives an incisive analysis of the crisis.

53. Text is in Browder and Kerensky, III, 1249–51.

54. Text of letter is in *ibid.*, p. 1252.

55. *Izvestiia*, No. 52, April 28; *Rech*, No. 97, April 27. The text of the letter to Chkheidze is in Browder and Kerensky, III, 1252–53.

56. See the editorials of *Delo Naroda* and *Volia Naroda* in Browder and Kerensky, III, 1256–58. See also Radkey, pp. 170–72.

57. Tsereteli, "Reminiscences," XV, 38–41. This is a translation of a part of his *Vospominaniia*. Voitinskii, in his manuscript (p. 102), states that Tsereteli was the most vigorous opponent of coalition.

58. Tsereteli ("Reminiscences," XV, 42–44) gives a good account of this meeting. For a press report, see *Russkiia Vedomosti*, No. 96, April 30, or the translation in Browder and Kerensky, III, 1267. The official minutes were in such bad condition they could not be reproduced. Pokrovskii and Iakovlev, I (*Protokoly*), 6.

59. Shulgin's speech is quoted in Browder and Kerensky, III, 1261–62.

60. Browder and Kerensky, III, 1263–65.

61. Texts of speeches are in Sack, pp. 287–91.

62. Guchkov, Nos. 5661 and 5668.

63. Tsereteli, *Vospominaniia*, I, 135.

64. *Ibid.*, pp. 135–36.

65. Pokrovskii and Iakovlev, I (*Protokoly*), 130–31: session of May 1. See also the account of Tsereteli, *Vospominaniia*, I, 136–37.

66. Tsereteli, *Vospominaniia*, I, 143–44; Miliukov, *Istoriia*, Part 1, pp. 110–11. The Soviet proposal was published along with the government proclamation in *Izvestiia*, No. 59, May 6.

67. Browder and Kerensky, III, 1277.

68. The negotiations can be pieced together from the accounts (though they are sometimes contradictory) of V. Nabokov, p. 64; Miliukov, *Istoriia*, Part 1, pp. 108–9; Stankevich, pp. 128–29; and Tsereteli, *Vospominaniia*, I, 143–64.

69. Tsereteli, *Vospominaniia*, I, 159–60; Gurevich, pp. 182–83.

CHAPTER IV

1. Browder and Kerensky, III, 1277. Relevant parts of the declaration are quoted on p. 48 above.

2. Tsereteli, *Vospominaniia*, I, 227–28, 349. Soviet leaders stressed that a basic reason for entering the government was to facilitate peace efforts, and that agreement to support a peace policy had been a condition for entry. See the May 9 speech of Liber in Goldman [Liber], p. 24, and Tsereteli's speech of May 7 to the All-Russian Conference of Mensheviks in *Rabochaia Gazeta*, No. 51, May 9.

3. *Rech*, No. 131, June 7.

4. On the activities of the Dutch-Scandinavian Committee and the reactions, see Fainsod, pp. 124–28; Gankin and Fisher, pp. 590–93; Meynell, Part 1, pp. 11–13.

5. On the Third Zimmerwald Conference, see Gankin and Fisher, pp. 582–682.

6. Pokrovskii and Iakovlev, IV (*Soveshchanie sovetov*), 95–97.

7. *Ibid.*, I (*Protokoly*), 101.

8. *Ibid.*, pp. 123–26; Tsereteli, *Vospominaniia*, I, 277–81.

9. Pokrovskii and Iakovlev, I (*Protokoly*), 127–28: session of April 25; *ibid.*, II (*Sezd sovetov*), Part 1, pp. 428–34: speech of Rozanov at the All-Russian Congress of Soviets, June 11.

10. *Ibid.*

11. The MacDonald letter and a letter from some Swedish pacifists are cited in Shliapnikov, IV, 28–31.

12. Vandervelde, "Rapport," pp. 34–35. The section in Vandervelde's *Three Aspects* entitled "Political Situation" follows this report closely, but omits some details that might have been considered important to the war or embarrassing to Allied leaders. Among the passages omitted is one that refers to Tsereteli as the dominant member of the Russian government.

13. The text of the appeal is in Golder, *Documents*, pp. 340–43.

14. *Ibid.*, pp. 397–99.

15. *Izvestiia*, No. 55, May 2.

16. *Ibid.*, No. 52, April 28. For the text of the telegram to the British government, see Lloyd George, IV, 1888. For the negative reaction of the British War Cabinet, see Great Britain, War Cabinet minutes, No. 1138, May 15, Cab. 23/2.

17. *Izvestiia*, No. 57, May 4.   18. Ribot, *Letters*, p. 232.

19. Hamilton, p. 132.   20. Vandervelde, "Rapport," p. 16.

21. Tsereteli, *Vospominaniia*, I, 211–12.

22. A list of articles is attached to Vandervelde, "Rapport."

23. War Cabinet minutes, No. 141, May 21, Cab. 23/2.

24. Tsereteli, *Vospominaniia*, I, 201. On the actions of British labor, see Lloyd George, IV, 1887–98; Hamilton, pp. 122–29; Graubard, pp. 23–25; and Warth, pp. 69–74.

25. Exchange quoted in Sack, pp. 364–67.
26. Stankevich, p. 108.
27. Pokrovskii and Iakovlev, I (*Protokoly*), 139.
28. The minutes of the two meetings are in Shliapnikov, IV, 34–35.
29. Pokrovskii and Iaklovlev, I (*Protokoly*), 153–54; *Izvestiia*, No. 70, May 19.
30. *Izvestiia*, No. 72, May 21.
31. France, *Journal Officiel* (1917), pp. 1323–24: Chambre des Députés, June 2.
32. France, *Journal Officiel* (May 16–19, 1925), pp. 495–99: secret session of June 1, 1917. The resolution, which was public, did not mention Stockholm or passports, the subject of the secret session, but was a vaguely worded salute to the Russian revolution and an assurance of the honorable and just aims of France in the war. For the text of the resolution, see *Journal Officiel* (1917), p. 1324.
33. A summary of the debates on these issues is in Tsereteli, *Vospominaniia*, I, 184–214.
34. Tsereteli, *Vospominaniia*, I, 205–11; Vandervelde, "Rapport," pp. 34–35.
35. Browder and Kerensky, II, 1173–74.
36. *Izvestiia*, No. 81, June 2; partially translated in Browder and Kerensky, II, 1174–75.
37. Rafael Abramovich, *Soviet Revolution*, p. 40.
38. Lenin, XXIV, 384.
39. Denicke, p. 42.
40. Trotsky, *History*, I, 454.
41. *Raionnye Sovety Petrograda*, I, 11–12.
42. *Rabochaia Gazeta*, Nos. 51–60, May 9–19; Voitinskii, manuscript, p. 116; Getzler, pp. 148–55.
43. See the account of the Bolsheviks' preparation for this triumph in Rabinowitch, pp. 97–106, and the documents in Browder and Kerensky, III, 1311–26.
44. Rozanov, *Democraticheskaia respublika*.
45. Voitinskii, *K chemu*, pp. 3–10.
46. Vodovozov. Vodovozov was a Defensist Menshevik and a frequent contributor to *Den*.
47. Voitinskii (manuscript, pp. 29–35, 108–10) described these meeting efforts and the problems created by the lack of contact of the soldiers and workers not only with the top Soviet leaders but with their own elected representatives in the Soviet. A delegate to the All-Russian Congress of Soviets, who was also chairman of the Luga Soviet, stressed this lack of contact as a major cause of the alienation of the

Petrograd masses from the Soviet leadership. See N. Voronovich, pp. 59–68.

48. *Delo Naroda,* No. 71, June 10.

49. Golder, *Documents,* p. 371. For the full text, see *ibid.,* pp. 360–71.

50. For the organization and early activities of the delegation, see Wade, "Argonauts," pp. 453–58.

51. Browder and Kerensky, II, 939.

52. *Novaia Zhizn,* No. 25, May 17, and *Izvestiia,* No. 68, May 17. *Novaia Zhizn,* an independent leftist paper edited by Maxim Gorky and Sukhanov, tended to express the views of the Menshevik-Internationalists.

53. For the text of Tsereteli's speech, see Golder, *Documents,* pp. 361–63.

54. Voitinskii, *K chemu,* pp. 3–10.

55. Voitinskii, manuscript, pp. 96–97, 114–15.

CHAPTER V

1. V. Nabokov, p. 45; Rodzianko, "Krushenie Imperii," pp. 157–58; Miliukov, *Istoriia,* Part 1, pp. 45–46.

2. Tsereteli, *Vospominaniia,* I, 160–61; Buchanan, II, 125. According to Tsereteli, Tereshchenko spelled out his views to him (emphasizing that he was not a socialist) during the government crisis, while he was still being considered for the post of Foreign Minister. Tereshchenko told Buchanan his views on the Straits as early as April 24.

3. United States, *Records,* File No. 861.00/362½; Great Britain, War Cabinet minutes, No. 146, May 25 (12), Cab. 23/2.

4. Buchanan, II, 128–29.

5. *Ibid.;* United States, *Papers, Russia,* I, 86–92.

6. Meeting reported in Abramovich, *Soviet Revolution,* pp. 43–45.

7. The text of the revised French note is in Browder and Kerensky, II, 1107–8. For the text of the original note, a copy of which was sent to the United States government, see United States, *Records,* File No. 861.00/374. The text of the Italian note is in Browder and Kerensky, II, 1108.

8. Browder and Kerensky, II, 1106–7. Since the British alone of the signatories of these treaties did not have contiguous territorial conquests at stake and were certainly willing to have Russia give up her prospective foothold on the Mediterranean, they could best afford to make such a concession.

9. Buchanan, II, 128–29, 133–34; Great Britain, War Cabinet minutes, No. 159, June 8 (May 26), Cab. 23/2.

10. For the negotiations, see United States, *Papers, Russia*, I, 86–94.

11. Daniels, pp. 158–59.

12. Charles Seymour, III, 37–51.

13. Great Britain, War Cabinet minutes, No. 187, July 16 (3), Cab. 23/2.

14. Tsereteli, *Vospominaniia*, I, 366–68.

15. Adamov, *Konstantinopol*, I, 498.

16. No. 67, May 28.

17. No. 78, May 30; partially translated in Browder and Kerensky, II, 1112.

18. *Ibid.*   19. *Ibid.*

20. *Ibid.*   21. No. 67, May 28.

22. No. 127, May 30.

23. Miliukov, *Istoriia*, I, pp. 166–85.

24. See the article by S. A. Klivanskii in *Den*, No. 71, May 30. This article was sent by the American consul in Petrograd, North Winship, to Secretary of State Lansing June 2/15. See United States, *Records*, File No. 861.00/438.

25. Text of speech is in Browder and Kerensky, II, 1083.

26. *Izvestiia*, No. 51, April 27.

27. *Den*, No. 54, May 9.

28. Chernov, *Great Revolution*, p. 194. This argument was repeated over and over, in both sophisticated and simplistic terms, in the speeches and writings of the Revolutionary Defensists.

29. As quoted in Browder and Kerensky, II, 1103–4.

30. The text of the proposal is in Golder, *Documents*, pp. 355–56.

31. Browder and Kerensky, II, 1121–22.

32. No. 72, June 4.

33. No. 129, June 4.

34. Voitinskii, *K chemu*, pp. 5–6.

35. *Russkiia Vedomosti*, No. 127, July 7. His comments were made available to high British officials through the British government's confidential press survey. See Great Britain, General Staff, *Review*, Series 3, June 22 (9), p. 531.

36. Great Britain, *Parliamentary Debates*, XCV, 179–80.

37. Browder and Kerensky, II, 1123.

38. May 21/June 3, in Adamov, *Konstantinopol*, I, 495.

39. Tsereteli, *Vospominaniia*, I, 371.

40. "Diplomatiia," p. 19.

41. Browder and Kerensky, III, 1277.

42. *Ibid.*, II, 935–36.

43. See text of speech in Kerensky, *Ob armii*, p. 11.

44. See, for example, Denikin, *Russian Turmoil*, p. 142.

45. Such sentiments are sprinkled throughout the works of the Soviet figures who wrote in 1917 or about the period. See, for example, *Izvestiia*, June 22 and June 30; *Rabochaia Gazeta*, June 20; *Delo Naroda*, June 20; and the speeches of Skobelev and Tsereteli to the Soviet printed in *Izvestiia*, May 2. For later analyses, see Stankevich, pp. 120–22; Chernov, *Great Revolution*, p. 299; and Kerensky, *Crucifixion*, pp. 330–40.

46. No. 98, June 22. See Browder and Kerensky, II, 944–50, for a sample of the socialist press reaction.

47. See Browder and Kerensky, II, 951–55; and Rabinowitch, pp. 109–10.

48. On the defeat of the army, the government crisis, and the July uprising in Petrograd, see the documents and brief narrative in Browder and Kerensky, II, 959–88, and III, 1331–1400; and Golder, *Documents*, pp. 425–64. For first-person accounts, see Sukhanov, *Russian Revolution*, pp. 424–82; Tsereteli, *Vospominaniia*, II, 259–345; Kerensky, *Catastrophe*, pp. 221–57; and Trotsky, *History*, II, 3–84. See Rabinowitch for a detailed and definitive account of the July crisis.

CHAPTER VI

1. Accounts of the July 21 meeting are in *Izvestiia*, Nos. 124–25, July 22–23, and *Rech*, Nos. 170–71, July 22–23. For a number of documents on the crisis see Browder and Kerensky, III, 1383–1436. A good discussion of the "coalition mentality" in Soviet circles may be found in David Anin, "The February Revolution: Was the Collapse Inevitable?" *Soviet Studies*, XVII, 4 (April 1967), 453–57.

2. Browder and Kerensky, III, 1430.

3. See the Nekrasov press statement on the new government in *Izvestiia*, No. 126, July 25.

4. *Rech*, No. 172, July 25.

5. Gessen, "V dvukh vekakh," p. 336. Gessen, the editor of *Rech*, attributes the statement to the period of the formation of the first coalition.

6. *Izvestiia*, No. 127, July 26. Unfortunately Tsereteli's memoirs leave off before this date. Nekrasov gave the same reason, adding that Tsereteli's decision "caused some friction." *Izvestiia*, No. 126, July 25.

7. Pokrovskii and Iakovlev, IX, is the stenographic account of the conference. Supplementary materials may be found in Browder and Kerensky, III, 451–522.

8. Text is in Browder and Kerensky, III, 1386–87.

9. *Ibid.*, II, 1122–23.

10. *Ibid.*, pp. 1123–24.

11. For the documents, see Ribot, *Journal*, p. 168; and Foch, p. 224. The editors of the Foch book mistakenly date this meeting as July 27 (14).

12. Great Britain, War Cabinet minutes, No. 200 A, July 31 (18), Cab. 23/13. (Meetings marked "A" were top secret.) A special memorandum the Imperial General Staff had prepared on the military implications of Russian defection was circulated.

13. C. Nabokoff (Konstantin Nabokov), *Ispytaniia diplomata*, pp. 106–10.

14. Great Britain, War Cabinet minutes, No. 203 A, Aug. 2 (July 20), Cab. 23/13.

15. Cited in Rubinshtein, p. 393.

16. Buchanan, II, 162–63; Pares, p. 468.

17. As quoted by Lockhart, "Unanimous Revolution," p. 329.

18. *Rech*, No. 184, Aug. 8.

19. *Zhurnaly*, Aug. 4, No. 147.

20. Buchanan to Balfour, Aug. 27/Sept. 8, "Inostrannye diplomaty," p. 158. Deciphered by Russian authorities.

21. On these maneuverings, see Adamov, *Razdel*, pp. 334–43, 510–13; Ribot, *Journal*, pp. 170–79; Adamov, *Konstantinopol*, II, 403–4; *Documents on British Foreign Policy* (London: H. M. Stationery Office, 1952), Series 1, IV, 639–42; United States, *Papers, Peace Conference*, V, 484, 720.

22. On Greek affairs, see Adamov, *Evropeiskie derzhavy*, pp. 190–212; *Rech*, Nos. 131 and 163, June 7 and July 11; *Zhurnaly*, No. 144, June 22, pp. 29–30; Great Britain, General Staff, *Review*, Series 3, July 11 (June 28), p. 644.

23. *New York Times*, July 30 (17), p. 2, and Aug. 1 (July 19), p. 2.

24. No. 3270, July 21; Adamov, *Konstantinopol*, I, 506–7.

25. Nos. 106–7, July 21–22.

26. No. 78, July 19. Article signed L. Martov.

27. Cited in Browder and Kerensky, II, 1126.

28. Telegram No. 4223, Sept. 11/24, cited in Browder and Kerensky, II, 1127. The full exchange is in Adamov, *Konstantinopol*, I, 508–12.

29. Adamov, *Konstantinopol*, I, 511–12.

30. Pokrovskii and Iakovlev, I (*Protokoly*), 268; Tsereteli, *Vospominaniia*, I, 301–5; Rusanov, pp. 4–5, 57. Rusanov's work, a memoir of the delegation, was written in the latter half of the 1930's at the suggestion of Boris Nicolaevsky.

31. Rusanov, pp. 24–28; and the report of the Soviet delegation

published in *Izvestiia*, July 1, 1917. A text of the report in Gankin and Fisher (pp. 637–40, "Report of the Foreign Delegation of the All-Russian Congress of Soviets") includes the slight differences found in "Fevralskaia revoliutsiia i evropeiskie sotsialisty," XVI, 27–29.

32. Text of the letter is in Shliapnikov, IV, 47; source for date is Tsereteli, *Vospominaniia*, I, 307.

33. The letter from Erlikh to Rozanov, July 21, is quoted in Shliapnikov, IV, 57.

34. Rusanov, pp. 39–60; *Izvestiia*, July 16.

35. *L'Humanité*, July 29 (16), 1917; Rusanov, pp. 71–80.

36. Report of Erlikh in *Izvestiia*, Sept. 10; *L'Humanité*, July 30, 31 (17, 18); Rusanov, pp. 78–89; Tsereteli, *Vospominaniia*, I, 319–21; Hamilton, pp. 137–38.

37. Great Britain, War Cabinet minutes, No. 196 A, July 26 (13), Cab. 23/13.

38. *Ibid.*, No. 199 A, July 30 (17).

39. *Ibid.*, No. 207, Aug. 8 (July 26), Cab. 23/3.

40. On the situation in London, see Lloyd George, IV, 1898–1924; Graubard, pp. 25–35; Hamilton, pp. 135–62; Meynell, pp. 203–5; Great Britain, *Parliamentary Debates*, XCVII, August 14 (1), pp. 909–34.

41. The text of the telegram is in C. Nabokoff (Konstantin Nabokov), *Ordeal*, pp. 134–36, along with his reasons for sending it.

42. *Ibid.*, pp. 138–39.

43. Great Britain, War Cabinet minutes, No. 211, Aug. 10 (July 28), Cab. 23/3.

44. C. Nabokoff, *Ordeal*, p. 140; Lloyd George, IV, 1914–24.

45. C. Nabokoff, *Ordeal*, pp. 139–40.

46. Great Britain, War Cabinet minutes, No. 212, Aug. 11 (July 29) and No. 213, Aug. 13 (July 31), Cab. 23/2.

47. *The Times* (London), Aug. 13 (July 31). See also C. Nabokoff, *Ordeal*, pp. 140–48).

48. Great Britain, *Parliamentary Debates*, XCVII, Aug. 13 (July 31), pp. 909–34.

49. For selections from the socialist papers of Aug. 2, see Great Britain, General Staff, *Review*, Series 4, Aug 18 (5), p. 135.

50. *Izvestiia*, No. 133, Aug. 2. The statement was reported to have come from "an authoritative source" and was headlined "The Provisional Government on the Stockholm Conference."

51. *Ibid.*, No. 134, Aug. 3.

52. Cited in C. Nabokoff, *Ordeal*, pp. 151–52.

53. No. 135, Aug. 4.

54. No. 125, Aug. 4.

55. No. 180, Aug. 3.

56. Buchanan, II, 164.

57. C. Nabokoff, *Ispytaniia diplomata*, p. 123.

58. Cited in *Izvestiia*, No. 239, Nov. 29.

59. Text of the deciphered telegraph is in Rubinshtein, pp. 433–34.

60. *Labour Leader*, Aug. 30 (17) and Sept. 6 (Aug. 24); *Report of the Labour Party*, pp. 8–11; *Pendant la guerre*, pp. 183–89; *L'Humanité*, Sept. 4 (Aug. 22); Rusanov, pp. 119–20. The meeting was closed to the public, and an account must be pieced together from scattered sources.

61. *Izvestiia*, No. 152, Aug. 24.

CHAPTER VII

1. For some details of the Kornilov affair, see the documents and bibliography in Browder and Kerensky, III, 1523–1612. See also White for a close analysis of the nature of Kornilov's support, Ascher for the generally accepted historical evaluation of the affair (unfavorable to Kornilov), and Strakovsky for a defense of Kornilov's actions.

2. Dan, p. 164; Chernov, *Ts. k-t P. S. R.*, p. 48.

3. *Rabochaia Gazeta*, Sept. 24; Lande, pp. 72–76; Zhordania, pp. 77–78. On the Socialist Revolutionaries, see Radkey, pp. 412–13.

4. The resolutions and votes are in Browder and Kerensky, III, 1685–86.

5. Voitinskii, manuscript, pp. 307–8.

6. *Izvestiia*, No. 193, Oct. 10.

7. Buchanan, II, 183: dispatch to the Foreign Ministry of Aug. 28/Sept. 10.

8. *Ibid.*, pp. 189–91; United States, *Records*, File No. 861.00/877: Francis to Lansing.

9. Buchanan, II, 183, 191.

10. United States, *Papers, Russia*, I, 196–97; Buchanan, II, 191; Noulens, I, 88.

11. Noulens, I, 88; United States, *Records*, File No. 861.00/559. Though no reply was sent, both Wilson and Lansing saw the ambassador's dispatch about the intended démarche.

12. Noulens, I, 89.

13. Buchanan, II, 190–91.

14. United States, *Papers, Russia*, I, 207–8. This draft is softened very slightly from that sent to Washington for approval (*ibid.*, pp. 196–97), but the two versions are essentially the same.

15. Noulens, I, 89.

16. *Ibid.*

17. Buchanan, II, 192–93; Noulens, I, 91–92.

18. United States, *Papers, Russia,* I, 207.

19. The texts of the three telegrams are in Browder and Kerensky, III, 1626–27.

20. The reports of Nabokov (London), Sevastopulo (Paris), and Giers (Rome) to Tereshchenko are in *Sbornik sekretnykh dokumentov,* pp. 110–13.

21. Noulens, I, 93.

22. Kerensky, *Crucifixion,* pp. 359–60.

23. The origins of the Pope's proposal are discussed in Forster, pp. 126–28.

24. On these efforts, and for information on the Prince Sixte negotiations, the so-called Armand-Revertera negotiations, and the von der Lancken affair, see *ibid.,* pp. 102–12.

25. Text in Browder and Kerensky, III, 1459.

26. United States, *Papers, World War,* I, 175: Sharp (U.S. ambassador to France) to Lansing, Aug. 11/24; Seymour, III, 155: Balfour to Colonel House, Aug. 9/22.

27. Forster, pp. 129–31.

28. Seymour, III, 157–58: House to Wilson.

29. United States, *Papers, World War,* I, 178–79.

30. Text of the Austrian and German notes in *ibid.,* pp. 217–20.

31. See text in Browder and Kerensky, III, 1164–65.

32. No. 180, Sept. 24.

33. No. 208, Sept. 12.

34. For his full press statement, see Browder and Kerensky, III, 1165–66.

35. Great Britain, General Staff, *Review,* Series 4, Sept. 27 (14), p. 462.

36. *Rech,* No. 221, Sept. 20.

37. Great Britain, War Cabinet minutes, No. 230, Sept. 10 (Aug. 28), Cab. 23/4.

38. The press discussion of a Japanese occupation of Siberia is extensively recorded in Great Britain, General Staff, *Review, Allied Supplement,* June 27 (14), p. 190, Aug. 29 (16), p. 303, Nov. 21 (8), pp. 81–82.

39. *Rech,* No. 218, Sept. 16; and *Russkiia Vedomosti,* No. 214, Sept. 20 (which is partly translated in Browder and Kerensky, II, 1166–68).

40. V. Nabokov, pp. 81–82; Nolde, "Nabokov," pp. 10–11.

41. V. Nabokov, p. 82. Nolde ("Nabokov," p. 11) says that Nabokov's account agrees with his own recollection of the meeting.

42. Ribot, *Journal*, p. 174.

43. Buchanan to Balfour, Aug. 23/Sept. 5, in "Inostrannye diplomaty," pp. 157–58. Deciphered by the Russian Foreign Ministry. The British conveyed the contents of this report by Buchanan to the United States in a memorandum. See United States, *Records*, File No. 861.00/501½.

44. Browder and Kerensky, III, 1714–15.

45. Verkhovskii, *Rossiia*, pp. 122–24.

46. Miliukov, *Istoriia*, Part 3, p. 151.

47. For the text of the instructions, see Browder and Kerensky, II, 1129–30.

48. *New York Times*, Nov. 1 (Oct. 19), p. 3.

49. C. Nabokoff, *Ordeal*, p. 166.

50. *Ibid.*; Cambon in the *New York Times*, Nov. 1 (Oct. 18), p. 3; Great Britain, *Parliamentary Debates*, XCVIII, 1187, 1447–48: Balfour to the House of Commons.

51. On the organization and functions of the Council of the Republic, see Gronsky and Astrov, pp. 105–10.

52. For the full text of the speech, see Browder and Kerensky, II, 1728–29.

53. "Nakanune," pp. 9–17; partially translated in Browder and Kerensky, II, 1130–35. This is a stenographic account of the session.

54. *Ibid.*, pp. 20–21.

55. *Ibid.*, p. 21.

56. *Ibid.*, p. 22; cited in Browder and Kerensky, II, 1137.

57. Text of speech is in Browder and Kerensky, II, 1138–44.

58. *Ibid.*, pp. 1144–47.

59. Voitinskii, manuscript, p. 326.

60. Buchanan, II, 190; Chernov, *Ts. k-t P. S. R.*, pp. 14–15; Knox, II, 695–96, 701.

61. Verkhovskii, *Rossiia*, p. 124.

62. V. Nabokov, pp. 80–83; Miliukov, *Istoriia*, Part 3, pp. 172–73; Slavin, p. 12.

63. Miliukov, *Istoriia*, Part 3, p. 172.

64. For a stenographic account of the session, see "Zhurnal." Much of that account is translated in Browder and Kerensky, III, 1735–43. This quotation is on p. 1738.

65. *Ibid.*, pp. 1738–39.

66. *Ibid.*, pp. 1740–42.

67. Voitinskii, manuscript, pp. 326–28.

68. Vinaver, p. 4; Miliukov, *Istoriia*, Part 3, pp. 175–76.

69. Verkhovskii, *Rossiia*, p. 138.
70. *Delo Naroda*, No. 187, Oct. 22.
71. *Ibid.*; Miliukov, *Istoriia*, Part 3, p. 176.
72. *Izvestiia*, Nos. 206 and 207, Oct. 25 and 26; Dan, pp. 172–75.
73. Gessen, "V dvukh vekakh," p. 377.

CHAPTER VIII

1. For an interesting essay on the fascination the French revolutions held for the Russian revolutionaries, see Keep, pp. 22–45.
2. V. Nabokov, p. 41.

BIBLIOGRAPHY

Bibliography

This bibliography is highly selective and represents only a fraction of the vast literature on the Russian revolution that I have consulted. Listed here are all the works cited in the Notes, together with others that I have found particularly helpful in furthering my understanding of the revolution. The listing is alphabetical for ease of reference from the short forms used in the notes. Contemporary newspapers are not listed here, and unless otherwise noted all newspapers cited in the notes are from the year 1917.

Abramovich, Rafael. "M. I. Liber," Za Svobodu, No. 18 (July 1947), 131–35.
———. The Soviet Revolution, 1917–1939. New York: International Universities Press, 1962.
Adamov, E. A., ed. Evropeiskie derzhavy i Gretsiia v epokhu Mirovoi Voiny po sekretnym dokumentam b. ministerstva inostrannykh del. Moskva: Narodnyi Komissariat Inostrannykh Del, 1922.
———. Konstantinopol i prolivy po sekretnym dokumentam b. ministerstva inostrannykh del. 2 vols. Moskva: Narodnyi Komissariat Inostrannykh Del, 1925.
———. Razdel Aziatskoi Turtsii po sekretnym dokumentam b. ministerstva inostrannykh del. Moskva: Narodnyi Komissariat Inostrannykh Del, 1924.
Alekseev, General M. V. "Iz dnevnika generala M. V. Alekseeva," in Ia. Ia. Slavik, ed., Russkii Istoricheskii Arkhiv, I (1929), 11–56.
Alekseev, S. A., ed. Revoliutsiia i grazhdanskaia voina v opisaniiakh belogvardeitsev. 5 vols. Moskva: Gosudarstvennoe Izdatelstvo, 1926.
Alexsinskii, G. A. Papers. Russian and East European Archive, Columbia University.
America's Message to the Russian People: Addresses by the Members of the Special Mission of the United States to Russia in the Year 1917. Boston: Marshall Jones, 1918.
Andreev, A. M. Sovety rabochikh i soldatskikh deputatov nakanune Oktiabria; Mart-oktiabr 1917 g. Moskva: Nauka, 1967.
Anet, Claude. La Révolution russe. 4 vols. Paris: Payot, 1918–19.
Anweiler, Oskar. Die Rätebewegung in Russland, 1905–1921. Leiden: Brill, 1958.

"Aprelskie dni 1917 goda v Petrograde," *Krasnyi Arkhiv*, XXX (1929), 34–81.

Aronson, Gregory. Rossiia v epokhu revoliutsii. New York: Waldon Press, 1966.

Artemev, S. A. "Sostav petrogradskoi Soveta v marte 1917 g.," *Istoriia SSSR*, 1964, No. 5, 112–28.

Ascher, Abraham. "The Kornilov Affair," *Russian Review*, XII, No. 4 (1953), 235–52.

Astrov, Nikolai, and Countess Sophia V. Panina. Papers. Russian and East European Archive, Columbia University.

Augustine, Wilson R. "Russia's Railwaymen, July-October, 1917" *Slavic Review*, XXIV, 4 (December 1965), 666–79.

Avrich, Paul H. "Russian Factory Committees in 1917," *Jahrbücher für Geschichte Osteuropas*, XI (1963), 161–82.

Baker, Ray Stannard. Woodrow Wilson, Life and Letters. 8 vols. New York: Doubleday, Doran, 1927–39.

Bakhmeteff, Boris A. Reminiscences. Oral History Project, Columbia University.

Balabanoff, Angelica. My Life as a Rebel. New York and London: Harper, 1938.

Baron, Samuel H. Plekhanov: the Father of Russian Marxism. Stanford, Calif.: Stanford University Press, 1963.

Billington, James. "Six Views of the Russian Revolution," *World Politics*, XVIII, 3 (April 1966), 452–73.

Boyd, John R. "The Origins of Order No. 1," *Soviet Studies*, XIX, 3 (January 1968), 359–72.

Browder, Robert Paul. "Kerenskij Revisited," *Harvard Slavic Studies*, IV (1957), 421–34.

Browder, Robert Paul, and Alexander Kerensky, eds. The Russian Provisional Government of 1917: Documents. 3 vols. Stanford, Calif.: Stanford University Press, 1961.

Brussilov, General A. A. A Soldier's Notebook 1914–1918. London: Macmillan, 1930.

Buchanan, Sir George. My Mission to Russia and Other Diplomatic Memories. 2 vols. London: Cassel, 1923.

Bukhbinder, N., ed. "Na fronte v predoktiabrskie dni: po sekretnym materialam Stavki," *Krasnaia Letopis'*, VI (1923), 9–63.

Bunyan, James, and H. H. Fisher, eds. The Bolshevik Revolution, 1917–1918: Documents and Materials. Stanford, Calif.: Stanford University Press, 1934.

Burdzhalov, E. N. Vtoraia russkaia revoliutsiia. Moskva: Nauka, 1967.

Cambon, Paul. Correspondance, 1870–1924. Edited by Henri Cambon. 3 vols. Paris: Editions Bernard Grasset, 1946.

Chamberlain, William Henry. The Russian Revolution, 1917–1921. 2 vols. New York: Macmillan, 1935.

Chernov, Victor (Viktor M.) The Great Russian Revolution. New Haven, Conn.: Yale University Press, 1936.

———. Pered Burei. New York: Chekhova, 1953.

———. Rozhdenie rcvoliutsionnoi Rossii. Paris, Prague, and New York: Iubileinyi Komitet po izdaniiu trudov V. M. Chernova, 1934.

———. Ts. k-t P. S. R. na rubezhe dvukh revoliutsii (kommentarii k protokolam tsentralnogo komiteta Partii sotsialistov-revoliutsionerov za period ot nachala sentiabria 1917 g. do ianvaria-fevralia 1918 g.). Manuscript, Hoover Institution, Stanford, Calif.

Chto takoe demokraticheskaia respublika? Moskva: "Prakticheskiia Znaniia," 1917.

Chto takoe demokraticheskaia respublika? Poiasnenie dlia grazhdan Rossii. Petrograd: Tip. gazety "Petrogradskii Listok," 1917.

Comité Organisateur de la Conférence Socialiste Internationale de Stockholm. Stockholm. Stockholm: Tidens Förlag, 1918.

Cross, Truman B. "Purposes of Revolution: Victor Chernov and 1917," Russian Review, XXVI, 4 (October 1967), 351–60.

Dan, F. "K istorii poslednikh dnei Vremennogo Pravitelstva," Letopis Revoliutsii, I (1923), 161–75.

Daniels, Josephus. The Cabinet Diaries of Josephus Daniels, 1913–1921. Edited by E. David Cronon. Lincoln: University of Nebraska Press, 1963.

Darling, William F. Diary. Hoover Institution, Stanford, Calif.

Denicke, George. Memoirs. Mimeographed manuscript, Nicolaevsky Collection, Hoover Institution, Stanford, Calif.

Denikin, General A. I. Ocherki Russkoi Smuty. 5 vols. Paris: J. Povolozky, 1921–26.

———. The Russian Turmoil: Memoirs Military, Social, and Political. London: Hutchinson, 1922.

Deutscher, Isaac. The Prophet Armed: Trotsky, 1879–1921. New York: Oxford University Press, 1954.

"Diplomatiia Vremennogo Pravitelstva v borbe s revoliutsiei," Krasnyi Arkhiv, XX (1927), 3–38.

Dobiash-Rozhdestvenskaia, O. A. Chto takoe Frantsiia v proshlom i nastoiashchem i za chto ona voiuet. Petrograd: Izdanie Partii Narodnoi Svobody, 1917.

Dosch-Fleurot, Arno. Through War to Revolution: Being the Experiences of a Newspaper Correspondent in War and Revolution, 1914–1920. London: John Lane, 1931.

Drachkovitch, Douchan. "Albert Thomas diplomate: Missions en Russie," Un grand citoyen du monde, Albert Thomas vivant:

Etudes, témoignages, souvenirs. Ouvrage publié par les soins de la Société des Amis d'Albert Thomas. Geneva: B. I. T., 1957.

Dvinov, Boris. "Moskovskii Sovet Rabochikh Deputatov 1917–1922; Vospominaniia." Inter-University Project on the History of the Menshevik Movement. Paper No. 1. New York, 1961.

——. "Pervaia mirovaia voina i rossiiskaia sotsialdemokratiia." Inter-University Project on the History of the Menshevik Movement. Paper No. 10. New York, 1961.

Ekonomicheskoe polozhenie Rossii nakanune Velikoi Oktiabrskoi sotsialisticheskoi revoliutsii. Edited by P. V. Volobuev. 2 vols. Moskva: Akademiia Nauk SSSR, 1957.

Epstein, Klaus. "The Development of German-Austrian War Aims in the Spring of 1917," *Journal of Central European Affairs,* XVII (April 1957), 23–47.

Ermanskii, Osip Arkadevich. Iz perezhitogo, 1887–1921. Moskva: Gosizdat, 1927.

Fainsod, Merle. International Socialism and the World War. Cambridge, Mass.: Harvard University Press, 1935.

Fedotoff White, D. Survival Through War and Revolution. Philadelphia: University of Pennsylvania Press, 1939.

Feldman, Robert S. "The Russian General Staff and the June 1917 Offensive," *Soviet Studies,* XIX, 4 (April 1968), 526–43.

Ferro, Marc. La Révolution de 1917: La chute du tsarisme et les origines d'Octobre. Paris: Aubier, Editions Montaigne, 1967.

——. "Les débuts du soviet de Petrograd," *Revue Historique,* CCXXIII (1960), 353–80.

"Fevralskaia revoliutsiia i evropeiskie sotsialisty," *Krasnyi Arkhiv,* XV (1926), 61–85; XVI (1926), 25–43.

"Fevralskaia revoliutsiia 1917 goda." *Krasnyi Arkhiv,* XXI (1927), 3–78; XXII (1927), 3–70.

Fischer, Fritz. Griff Nach der Weltmacht; Die Kriegszielpolitik des kaiserlichen Deutschland 1914/18. Dusseldorf: Droste Verlag, 1962.

Fischer, Louis. The Life of Lenin. New York: Harper, 1964.

Fishgendler, A. M. Soldaty fronta i voprosy voiny i mira. Petrograd: "Kniga," 1917.

Foch, Ferdinand. The Memoirs of Ferdinand Foch. Garden City, N.Y.: Doubleday, Doran, 1931.

Forster, Kent. The Failures of Peace: The Search for a Negotiated Peace During the First World War. Philadelphia: University of Pennsylvania Press, 1941.

France. *Journal Officiel de la République Française.* Paris, 1917.

——. *Journal Officiel de la République Française, débats parlementaires.* Paris, May 16–19, 1925.

Francis, David R. Papers. Missouri State Historical Society.

———. Russia from the American Embassy: April 1916–November 1918. New York: Scribner's, 1921.

Gankin, Olga, and H. H. Fisher, eds. The Bolsheviks and the World War. The Origin of the Third International. Stanford, Calif.: Stanford University Press, 1940.

Garvi, Petr A. "Iz vospominanii o fevralskoi revoliutsii," Sotsialisticheskii Vestnik, No. 702–3 (February-March 1957), 46–49.

———. Professionalnye soiuzy v Rossii v pervye gody revoliutsii. Edited and introduction by G. Aronson. New York: n.p, 1958.

———. Rabochaia kooperatsiia v pervye gody russkoi revoliutsii, 1917–1921. Manuscript, Nicolaevsky Collection, Hoover Institution, Stanford, Calif.

———. "Revoliutsionnye siluety." Inter-University Project on the History of the Menshevik Movement. Paper No. 2. New York, 1962.

Gessen, Iosif Vladimirovich. Memoirs; bibliography and author's corrections and instructions to the translator. Hoover Institution, Stanford, Calif.

———. "V dvukh vekakh," Arkhiv Russkoi Revoliutsii, XXII (1937), 3–424.

Getzler, Israel. Martov: A Political Biography of a Russian Social Democrat. Cambridge, Eng.: Cambridge University Press, 1967.

Geyer, Dietrich. Die Russische Revolution; Historische Probleme und Perspektiven. Stuttgart: W. Kohlhammer Verlag, 1968.

Globachev, General Konstantin I. Pravda o russkoi revoliutsii. Manuscript memoir, Russian and East European Archive, Columbia University.

Goldenweiser, Alexis. "Paul Miliukov—Historian and Statesman," Russian Review, XVI, 2 (1957), 3–14.

Golder, Frank A. Letter from Dr. Golder relating to Russian emigrés. Hoover Institution, Stanford, Calif.

———, ed. Documents of Russian History, 1914–1917. New York: Century Company, 1927.

Goldman [Liber], M. Zadachi rabochago klassa v russkoi revoliutsii. Moskva: Izd. E. D. Trautskoi, 1917.

Golovin, General N. N. Rossiiskaia kontr-revoliutsiia v 1917–1918 gg. 5 vols. Estonia: prilozhe k "Illiustrirovannoi Rossii," 1937.

———. The Russian Army in the World War. New Haven, Conn.: Yale University Press, 1931.

Gorin, P. O., ed. Organizatsiia i stroitelstvo sovetov RD v 1917 gody; Sbornik dokumenty. Moskva: Izdatelstvo Kommunisticheskoi Akademii, 1928.

Gourko, General Basil. War and Revolution in Russia, 1914–1917. New York: Macmillan, 1919.

Graubard, Stephen Richard. British Labour and the Russian Revolution, 1917–1924. Cambridge, Mass.: Harvard University Press, 1956.

Gronsky, Paul P., and Nicholas J. Astrov. The War and the Russian Government. New Haven, Conn.: Yale University Press, 1929.

Great Britain. General Staff, War Office. Daily Review of the Foreign Press. Series 2–5. London, 1917.

———. ———. Daily Review of the Foreign Press: Allied Press Supplement. Vols. I–III. London, 1917.

———. ———. Daily Review of the Foreign Press: Confidential Supplement. London, 1918.

———. House of Commons. Parliamentary Debates. Fifth Series, Vols. XCI–XCVIII. London: H. M. Stationery Office, 1917.

———. War Cabinet. Minutes of the War Cabinet. London, Public Record Office Microfilm.

Guchkov, A. I. "Iz Vospominanii A. I. Guchkova," Posledniia Novosti. Nos. 5654, 5658, 5661, 5665, 5668, September–October, 1936. Paris.

Gurevich, V. "Vserossiiskii Krestianskii Sezd i pervaia koalitsiia," Letopis Revoliutsii, I (1923), 176–96.

Hamilton, Mary Agnes. Arthur Henderson. London: William Heinemann, 1938.

Hanbury-Williams, Major-General Sir John: The Emperor Nicholas II as I Knew Him. London: Arthur L. Humphreys, 1922.

Hard, William. Raymond Robins' Own Story. New York: Harper, 1920.

Harper, Samuel N. Papers. University of Chicago Library.

———. The Russia I Believe In: The Memoirs of Samuel N. Harper; 1902–1941. Chicago: University of Chicago Press, 1945.

Iazvitskii, Valerii I. Kak narod dobilsia svoikh prav.—Kak zakrepit svobodu. Moskva: Izd. D. Iu. Makovskago, 1917.

Ignatev, A. V. "Bankrotstvo vneshnei politiki Vremennogo pravitelstva," Voprosy Istorii, 1967, No. 3, 3–16.

———. Russko-angliiskie otnosheniia nakanune Oktiabrskoi revoliutsii (fevral–oktiabr 1917 g.). Moskva: Nauka, 1966.

"Inostrannye diplomaty o revoliutsii 1917 g.," Krasnyi Arkhiv, XXIV (1927), 108–63.

Institute Izucheniia Rossii, Prague. Zapiski. 2 vols. Prague: n.p., 1925.

Ioffe, A. E. "Missiia Ruta v Rossii v 1917 gody," Voprosy Istorii, 1958, No. 9, 87–100.

Iurenev, I. "Mezhraionka, 1911–1917 gg.," Proletarskaia Revoliutsiia, No. 1 (24), 1924, pp. 109–39, and No. 2 (25), 1924, pp. 114–43.

"Iz dnevnika gen. V. G. Boldyreva," *Krasnyi Arkhiv*, XXIII (1927), 250–73.

Jessup, Philip. Elihu Root. 2 vols. New York: Dodd, Mead, 1938.

Judson, William V. Papers. Newberry Library, Chicago.

Katkov, George. "German Foreign Office Documents on Financial Support to the Bolsheviks in 1917," *International Affairs*, XXXII, 2 (1956), 181–89.

————. Russia, 1917: The February Revolution. New York: Harper, 1967.

Kazovskaia, A. "Nota Miliukova i aprelskie dni," *Proletarskaia Revoliutsiia*, No. 4 (63), 1927, 83–100.

Keep, J. L. H. "1917: The Tyranny of Paris over Petrograd," *Soviet Studies*, XX, 1 (July 1968), 22–45.

Kerensky, Alexander. The Catastrophe. Kerensky's Own Story of the Russian Revolution. New York: D. Appleton, 1934.

————. The Crucifixion of Liberty. New York: John Day, 1934.

————. "The February Revolution Reconsidered." Transcript of a radio interview of Alexander Kerensky by Leonard Schapiro, March 12, 1957. Annotated mimeograph copy in Hoover Institution, Stanford, Calif.

————. Izdaleka: Sbornik Statei (1920–1921 g.). Paris: Russkoe Knigoizdatelstvo Ia. Povolotskago, 1922.

————. Ob armii i voine. Petrograd: "Narodnaia Volia," 1917.

————. "The Policy of the Provisional Government of 1917," *The Slavonic and East European Review*, XI, 3 (1932), 1–19.

————. The Prelude to Bolshevism: The Kornilov Rising. New York: Dodd, Mead, 1919.

————. La Révolution russe, 1917. Paris: Payot, 1928.

————. Russia and History's Turning Point. New York: Duell, Sloan and Pearce, 1965.

Kerner, Robert J. "Russia and the Straits Question, 1915–17," *The Slavonic Review*, VIII (1930), 589–600.

Khodorovskii, Iosia I. Organizatsiia revoliutsionnykh sil. Vremennoe pravitelstvo, Sovety rabochikh, soldatskikh i krestianskikh deputatov. Moskva: "Obnovlenie," 1917.

Knox, Major-General Sir Alfred. With the Russian Army, 1914–1917; Being Chiefly Extracts from the Diary of a Military Attaché. 2 vols. London: Hutchinson, 1921.

Kochan, Lionel. "Kadet Policy in 1917," *Slavonic and East European Review*, XLV, 104 (January 1967), 183–92.

Korostovetz, Vladimir. Seed and Harvest. London: Faber and Faber, 1931.

Krupskaia, Nadezhda. Memories of Lenin. New York: International Publishers, 1930.

Krylenko, N. V. Pochemu pobezhala russkaia revoliutsionnaia armia. Petrograd: 1917.

Ladyzhenskii, A. M. Vneshnaiia politika i narodnoe predstavitelstvo. Moskva: D. Ia. Makovskii, 1917.

Lande, L. Menshevism v 1917 godu. Manuscript prepared for the Inter-University Project on the History of the Menshevik Movement.

Lansing, Robert. War Memoirs. New York: Bobbs-Merrill, 1935.

Lenin, V. I. Collected Works, Vols. XXIII–XXVI. Moscow: Progress Publishers, 1964.

Letuchii listok Menshevikov-internatsionalistov. No. 1; May 1917. Petrograd.

Liubarskii, B. Kakogo mira khochet trudovoi narod. Petrograd: n.p., 1917.

———. Komu dolzhen verit trudovoi narod. Petrograd: n.p., 1917.

Lloyd George, David. War Memoirs of David Lloyd George. 6 vols. London: Ivor Nicholson and Watson, 1934.

Lockhart, Sir Robert H. Bruce. British Agent. Garden City, N.Y.: Garden City Publishing Co., 1933.

———. "The Unanimous Revolution," Foreign Affairs, XXXV (January 1957), 320–33.

Long, Robert Crozier. Russian Revolution Aspects. New York: Dutton, 1919.

Loukomsky, General A. S. Memoirs of the Russian Revolution. London: T. Fisher Unwin, 1922.

Maklakov, V. A. Iz vospominanii. New York: Chekhova, 1954.

Mantayer, Georges de. Austria's Peace Offer, 1916–1917. London: Constable, 1921.

"Mart-mai 1917 g.," Krasnyi Arkhiv, XV (1926), 31–60.

Mayer, Arno. Political Origins of the New Diplomacy, 1917–18. New Haven, Conn.: Yale University Press, 1959.

Melgunov, S. P. Kak bolsheviki zakhvatili vlast: Oktiabrskii perevorot 1917 goda. Paris: "La Renaissance," 1953.

———. Martovskie dni 1917 goda. Paris: "Les Editeurs Réunis," 1961.

———. Sudba imperatora Nikolaia II posle otrecheniia. Paris: "La Renaissance," 1951.

Meynell, Hildamarie. "The Stockholm Conference of 1917," International Review of Social History, V (1960), 1–25, 202–25.

Michelson, Alexander, Paul Apostol, and Michael Bernatzky. Russian Public Finance During the War. New Haven, Conn., Yale University Press, 1928.

Miliukov, P. N. From Nicholas II to Stalin (Half-a-Century of Foreign Politics). Undated manuscript [?1941], Hoover Institution, Stanford, Calif.
———. Istoriia vtoroi russkoi revoliutsii. 1 vol. in 3 parts. Sofia: Rossiisko-Bolgarskoe Knigoizdatelstva, 1921–23.
———. "Konstantinopol i Prolivy," Vestnik Evropy, III, Bks. 1–6 (January–June 1917), 354–81, 227–59, 525–47.
———. Rossiia v plenu u tsimmervalda. Petrograd: "Svoboda," 1917.
———. Vospominaniia, 1859–1917. 2 vols. New York: Chekhova, 1955.
Mints, I. I. Istoriia velikogo oktiabria. Vols. I and II. Moskva: Nauka, 1967–68.
———. "Obrazovanie sovetov (fevral–mart 1917 g.)," Istoriia SSSR, 1967, No. 1, 3–17.
———. "Pervyi krizis vlast v aprele 1917 g. v Rossii," Voprosy Istorii, 1967, No. 1, 3–26.
Mstislavskii, S. Piat Dnei—Nachalo i Konets Fevralskoi Revoliutsii. Berlin, St. Petersburg, and Moscow: Izdatelstvo Z. I. Grzhebin, 1922.
Nabokoff, Constantin [Konstantin Nabokov]. The Ordeal of a Diplomat. London: Duckworth, 1921.
———. Ispytaniia diplomata. Stockholm: Severnyc Ogni, 1921.
Nabokov, Vladimir. "Vremennoe Pravitelstvo," Arkhiv Russkoi Revoliutsii, I (1920), 9–96.
"Nakanune oktiabrskago perevorota: Vopros o voine i mire; Otchety o sekretnykh zasedaniiakh komissii Vremennago Soveta Rossiiskoi Respubliki," Byloe, 1918, No. 6, 3–41.
Nekludoff, A. Diplomatic Reminiscences Before and During the World War, 1911–1917. London: John Murry, 1920.
Nikolaevskii [Nicolaevsky], B. I. Gruppa "Sibirskikh Tsimervaldistov." Manuscript, Nicolaevsky Collection, Hoover Institution, Stanford, Calif.
———. "I. G. Tsereteli," Sotsialisticheskii Vestnik, No. 730 (June 1959), 119–22; No. 731 (July 1959), 141–43; No. 732–33 (August–September 1959), 159–63; No. 734 (October 1959), 196–200; No. 735 (November 1959), 219–22; No. 736 (December 1959), 243–45; No. 738–39 (February–March 1960), 49–52.
———. "I. G. Tsereteli i ego vospominaniia o 1917 g.," Sotsialisticheskii Vestnik, No. 768 (August 1962), 110–14; No. 769–70 (September–October 1962), 132–36.
———. R. S. D. R. P. (Mensheviki) v pervye gody revoliutsii. Manuscript, Nicolaevsky Collection, Hoover Institution, Stanford, Calif.
———. "V. S. Voitinskii," Sotsialisticheskii Vestnik, No. 744–45 (August–September 1960), 165–69.

180 BIBLIOGRAPHY

Nikitine, Colonel B. V. The Fatal Years: Fresh Revelations on a Chapter of Underground History. London: William Hodge, 1938.

Nolde, Baron Boris. Dalekoe i blizkoe. Paris: Izd. "Sovremennyia Zapiski," 1930.

———. Russia in the Economic War. New Haven, Conn.: Yale University Press, 1928.

———. "V. D. Nabokov v 1917 g.," Arkhiv russkoi revoliutsii, VII (1922), 5–13.

Noulens, Joseph. Mon ambassade en Russie soviétique, 1917–1919. 2 vols. Paris: Librairie Plon, 1933.

Owen, Lancelot A. The Russian Peasant Movement, 1906–1917. New York: Russell and Russell, 1963.

Oznovishin, D. V. "O popytkakh Vremennogo pravitelstva Rossii reorganizovat armiiu," Istoricheskii Arkhiv, 1961, No. 4, 88–112.

Padenie tsarskogo rezhima: Stenograficheskie otchety doprosov i pokazanii dannykh v 1917 g. v Chrezvychainoi sledstvennoi komissii Vremennogo Pravitelstva. 7 vols. Leningrad: Gosudarstvennoe Izdatelstvo, 1924–27.

Paléologue, Maurice. An Ambassador's Memoirs. 3 vols. London: Hutchinson, 1923–25.

Painlevé, Paul. Comment j'ai nommé Foch et Pétain: La politique de guerre de 1917. Paris: Librairie Felix Alcan, 1924.

Pares, Bernard. My Russian Memoirs. London: Jonathan Cape, 1931.

Partiia sotsialistov revoliutsionerov. Tretii sezd Partii sotsialistov revoliutsionerov. Petrograd: Izd. Tsentral Komiteta P.S.R., 1917.

Pendant la guerre: le Parti Socialiste, la guerre et la paix. Paris: Librairie de l'Humanité, 1918.

"Perepiska Miliukova i Tereshchenko s poslami Vremennogo pravitelstva," Borba Klassov, No. 5 (1931), 84–88.

Peshekhonov, A. "Pervyia nedeli; iz vospominanii o revoliutsii," Na Chuzhoi Storone, I (1923), 255–319.

Piontkovskii, S. A. Krestomatiia po istorii Oktiabrskoi revoliutsii. 2d ed. Moskva: Krasnaia nov, 1924.

Pipes, Richard, ed. Revolutionary Russia. Cambridge, Mass.: Harvard University Press, 1968.

Plekhanov, Georgii Valentinovich. God na rodinie. Polnoe sobranie statei i riechi, 1917–1918 g. 2 vols. Paris: J. Povolozky, 1921.

Poincaré, Raymond. Au service de la France: neuf années de souvenirs. 10 vols. Paris: Librairie Plon, 1926–33.

Pokrovskii, M. N., ed. Ocherki po istorii Oktiabrskoi revoliutsii. 2 vols. Moskva: Gosizdat, 1927.

Pokrovskii, M. N., and Ia. A. Iakovlev, eds. *1917 god v dokumentakh i materialakh*. 10 vols. Moskva: Gosudarstvennoe Izdatelstvo, 1925–39.

    I. Petrogradskii sovet rabochikh i soldatskikh deputatov; protokoly zasedanii ispolnitelnogo komiteta i buiro I. K. 1925.

    II. Pervyi vserossiiskii sezd sovetov rabochikh i soldatskikh deputatov. 2 parts. 1930–31.

    III. Vtoroi vserossiiskii sezd sovetov rabochikh i soldatskikh deputatov. 1928.

    IV. Vserossiiskoe soveshchanie sovetov rabochikh i soldatskikh deputatov. 1927.

    V. Krestianskoe dvizhenie v 1917 godu. 1927.

    VI. Razlozhenie armii v 1917 godu. 1925.

    VII. Rabochee dvizhenie v 1917 godu. 1926.

    VIII. Burzhuaziia nakanune fevralskoi revoliutsii. 1927.

    IX. Gosudarstvennoe Soveshchanie. 1939.

    X. Vserossiiskoe Uchreditelnoe Sobranie. 1930.

Polner, Tikon I. Zhiznennyi put Kniazia Georgiia Evgenievicha Lvova. Paris: n.p., 1932.

Poole, DeWitt Clinton. Papers. Wisconsin State Historical Society.

————. Reminiscences. Oral History Project, Columbia University.

Popova, E. I. "Missiia Stivensa i proval zheleznodorozhnoi politiki S. Sh. A. v rossii i kitae v 1917–1922 gg.," *Istoricheskie Zapiski*, LX (1957), 31–85.

Potresov, A. N. Posmertnyi sbornik proizvedenii. Paris: Dom Knigi, 1937.

Price, M. Philips. My Reminiscences of the Russian Revolution. London: Allen and Unwin, 1921.

Rabinowitch, Alexander. Prelude to Revolution: The Petrograd Bolsheviks and the July 1917 Uprising. Bloomington: Indiana University Press, 1968.

Radkey, Oliver H. The Agrarian Foes of Bolshevism: Promise and Default of the Russian Socialist Revolutionaries, February to October, 1917. New York: Columbia University Press, 1953.

Rafailov-Chernyshev, Val. Kto za svobodu, tot za pobedu. Petrograd: Izd. otdel Tsentralnogo voenno-promyshlennago komiteta, 1917.

Rafes, M. "Moi vospominaniia," *Byloe*, 1922, No. 19, 177–97.

Raionnye Sovety Petrograda v 1917 godu. 3 vols. Moskva: Nauka, 1964.

Report of the Seventeenth Annual Conference of the Labour Party. London, 1918.

Revoliutsiia 1917 goda; Khronika sobytii. N. Avdeev et al., eds. 6 vols. Moskva: Gosizdat, 1923–30.

Ribot, Alexandre. Journal et correspondances inédites, 1914–1922. Paris: Librairie Plon, 1936.

———. Letters to a Friend: Recollections of My Political Life. London: Hutchinson, 1924.

Riha, Thomas. "1917—A Year of Illusions," Soviet Studies, XIX, 1 (July 1967), 115–21.

———. A Russian European: Paul Miliukov in Russian Politics. Notre Dame, Ind.: University of Notre Dame Press, 1969.

Robien, Louis de. Journal d'un diplomate en Russie, 1917–1918. Paris: Editions Albin Michel, 1967.

Robins, Raymond. Papers. Wisconsin State Historical Society.

Rodichev, Fedor I. Vospominaniia o 1917 g. Typed manuscript, Hoover Institution, Stanford, Calif.

Rodzianko, M. V. "Gosudarstvennaia Duma i fevralskaia 1917 goda revoliutsiia," Arkhiv Russkoi Revoliutsii, VI (1922), 5–81.

———. "Krushenie Imperii," Arkhiv Russkoi Revoliutsii, XVII (1925), 5–170.

"Romanovy i Soiuzniki v pervie dni revoliutsii," Krasnyi Arkhiv, XVI (1926), 44–52.

Rosen, Baron Roman. Forty Years of Diplomacy. 2 vols. London: Allen and Unwin, 1922.

Rosenberg, William G. "Les Libéraux russes et le changement de pouvoir en mars, 1917, Cahiers du Monde Russe et Sovietique, IX, 1 (January 1968), 46–57.

Routsky, Pierre. "A Page from the Past," Russian Review, VII, 2 (1948), 69–75.

Rozanov, V. Demokraticheskaia respublika i mir. Petrograd: "Kniga," 1917. Pamphlet, published in late May or early June.

———. Organizatsiia verkhovnoi vlasti. Petrograd: "Kniga," 1917.

———. Proiskhozhdenie voiny. Moskva: "Knigoizdatelstvo Pisatelei," 1917.

Rohzkov, Nikolai Aleksandrovich. Proiskhozhdenie i khod russkoi revoliutsii. Moskva: Izd-vo "Soldat-grazhdanin," 1917.

Rubinshtein, N. L. "Vneshniaia politika Kerenshchiny," in M. N. Pokrovskii, ed., Ocherki, listed above. Vol. II, 349–452.

Rusanov, N. S. Argonavty mira. Manuscript, Nicolaevsky Collection, Hoover Institution, Stanford, Calif.

Russia. Provisional Government. Osobyi Zhurnal Zasedaniia Vremennago Pravitelstva 1917. Petrograd, 1917.

———. Zhurnaly Zasedanii Vremennago Pravitelstva. 2 vols. Petrograd, 1917.

————. Zhurnaly Zasedanii Vremennago Pravitelstva, Proekt. Petrograd, 1917.

Sack, A. J., ed. The Birth of the Russian Democracy. New York: Russian Information Bureau, 1918.

Sbornik sekretnykh dokumentov iz arkhiva byvshago ministerstva inostrannykh del. Petrograd: Izdanie Komissariata po Inostrannym delam, 1917.

Schaper, B. W. Albert Thomas: trente ans de réformisme social. Assen: Van Gorcum, 1959.

Schatzky, B. E. "La Révolution russe de février 1917 et les États-Unis d'Amerique," Monde slave, V (1928), 353–76.

Serezhnikov, Viktor K. Kak ukrepit novye poriadki. Moskva: Sotsial-Demokraticheskoe Izd. "Delo," 1917.

Seymour, Charles, ed. The Intimate Papers of Colonel House. 4 vols. Boston: Houghton Mifflin, 1928.

Shestakov, A. V., ed. Sovety krestianskikh deputatov i drugie krestianskie organizatsii. 1 vol. in 2 parts. Moskva: Izd. Kommunisticheskoi Akademii, 1929.

Shidlovskii, S. I. Vospominaniia. 2 vols. Berlin: Otto Kirchner, 1923.

Shliapnikov, Aleksandr G. Semnadtsatyi god. 4 vols. Moskva: Gosizdat, 1923–31.

Shteinberg, I. Ot fevralia po oktiabr 1917 g. Berlin and Milan: Izdatelstvo "Skify," 1920.

Shub, David. Lenin, a Biography. Garden City, N.Y.: Doubleday, 1949.

Shulgin, V. V. Dni. Belgrade: Novoe Vremia, 1925.

Slavin, N. F. "Iz istorii krizisa verkhov nakanune Oktiabrskoi revoliutsii," Istoriia SSSR, 1964, No. 6, 3–21.

Smirnov, A. S. "Petrogradskii Sovet Krestianskikh Deputatov v 1917 g.," Istoricheskie Zapiski, No. 73 (1963), 90–110.

Smith, C. Jay, Jr. "Miliukov and the Russian National Question," Harvard Slavic Studies, IV (1957), 394–419.

————. The Russian Struggle for Power, 1914–1917. New York: Philosophical Library, 1956.

Smith, Nathan. "The Role of Russian Freemasonry in the February Revolution: Another Scrap of Evidence," Slavic Review, XXVII, 4 (December 1968), 604–8.

Snell, John. "The Russian Revolution and the German Social Democratic Party in 1917," The American Slavic and East European Review, XV (1956), 351–63.

Solovev, Iu. Ia. Vospominaniia diplomata, 1893–1922. Moskva: Izdatelstvo sotsialno-ekonomicheskoi literaturi, 1959.

Sorokin, Pitirim. Leaves from a Russian Diary. New York: Dutton, 1924.

Spiridovich, General A. I. Velikaia Voina i Fevralskaia Revoliutsiia, 1914–1917. 3 vols. New York: Vseslavianskoe Izdatelstvo, 1962.

Stankevich, V. B. Vospominaniia 1914–1919. Berlin: Izdatelstvo E. P. Ladyzhnikov, 1920.

"Stavka i ministerstvo inostrannykh del," Krasnyi Arkhiv, XXX (1930), 5–45.

Steklov, Iurii M. Mezhdunarodnaia politika rabochago klassa. Petrograd: "Zhizn i znanie," 1917.

———. Vospominaniia i publitsistika. Moskva: Izvestiia, 1965.

Stevens, John. Papers. Hoover Institution, Stanford, Calif.

Strakhovsky, Leonid. "Was There a Kornilov Rebellion?—A Re-appraisal of the Evidence," The Slavonic and East European Review, XXXIII (1955), 372–95.

Sukhanov, N. N. The Russian Revolution, 1917. Edited, abridged, and translated by Joel Carmichael. London: Oxford University Press, 1955.

———. Zapiski o revoliutsii. 7 vols. Berlin, St. Petersburg, and Moscow: Izdatelstvo Z. I. Grzhebina, 1922.

Szporluk, Roman. "Pokrovskii's View of the Russian Revolution," Slavic Review, XXVI, 1 (March 1967), 71–83.

Tainye dokumenty iz arkhiva russkago ministerstva inostrannykh del. Moskva: Ministerstvo Inostrannykh Del, 1918.

Tereshchenko, M. I. "Ekaterinburgskaia tragediia," Posledniia Novosti, No. 4108 (June 21, 1932).

Thorne, Will. My Life's Battles. London: George Newnes, 1925.

Trotsky, Leon. The History of the Russian Revolution. 3 vols. New York: Simon and Schuster, 1936.

———. Sochineniia. Vol. III. Moskva: Gosizdat, 1925.

Tsereteli [Tseretelli], I. G. "Reminiscences of the February Revolution: The April Crisis," Russian Review, XIV (1955), 93–108, 184–200, 301–21; XV (1956), 37–48.

———. Vospominaniia o fevralskoi revoliutsii. 2 vols. Paris: Mouton, 1963.

Ulam, Adam B. The Bolsheviks. New York: Macmillan, 1965.

United States. Department of State. Records of the Department of State Relating to Internal Affairs of Russia and the Soviet Union, 1910–29. National Archives Microfilm Publications, No. 316, 180 reels. Washington: National Archives and Records Service, 1960. State Department File No. 861.

———. Records of the Department of State Relating to Political Relations Between Russia and the Soviet Union and Other States, 1910–29. National Archives Microfilm Publications, No. 340, 20 reels. Washington: National Archives and Record Service, 1961. State Department File No. 761.

———. Records of the Department of State Relating to Political Relations Between the United States and Russia and the Soviet Union, 1910–29. National Archives Microfilm Publications, No. 333, 7 reels. Washington: National Archives and Records Service, 1960. State Department File No. 711.61.

———. Papers Relating to the Foreign Relations of the United States, 1918, Russia. 3 vols. Washington: Government Printing Office, 1931.

———. Papers Relating to the Foreign Relations of the United States, 1917, Supplement 2, the World War. 2 vols. Washington: Government Printing Office, 1932.

———. Papers Relating to the Foreign Relations of the United States: The Lansing Papers, 1914–1920. 2 vols. Washington: Government Printing Office, 1939–40.

———. Papers Relating to the Foreign Relations of the United States: The Paris Peace Conference, 1919. 11 vols. Washington: Government Printing Office, 1942.

Van Der Slice, Austin. International Labor, Diplomacy, and Peace, 1914–1919. Philadelphia: University of Pennsylvania Press, 1941.

Vandervelde, Emile. Rapport sur la mission accomplie en Russie, de mai à juillet 1917, par Monsieur le Ministre Vandervelde, M. Louis de Brouckère, et le lieutenant Henri de Man. This report, which was delivered to the American minister to Belgium, may be found in Annex to State Department File No. 861.00/565, United States, Department of State, Records of the Department of State Relating to Internal Affairs of Russia and the Soviet Union, 1910–1929. National Archives Microfilm Publication No. 316.

———. Three Aspects of the Russian Revolution. New York: Scribner's, 1918.

Vasiukov, V. S. Vneshniaia politika Vremennogo pravitelstva. Moskva: Mysl, 1966.

Velikaia oktiabrskaia sotsialisticheskaia revoliutsiia: Dokumenty i materialy. 7 vols. Moskva: Izdatelstvo Akademii Nauk SSSR, 1957–61.

Verkhovskii, General A. I. Na trudnom perevale. Moskva: War Ministry Publishing House, 1959.

———. Rossiia na Golgof; iz pokhodnago dnevnika 1914–1918 g. Petrograd: "Delo Naroda," 1918.

Vinaver, M. M. "V te dni," Posledniia Novosti, No. 478 (November 6, 1921), 3–4.

Vishniak, Mark. Dan Proshlomu. New York: Chekhov, 1954.

———. Dva puti (Fevral i Oktiabr). Paris: Izd. Sovremennyia Zapiski, 1931.

Vodovozov, V. V. Chto takoe mir bez anneksii i kontributsii? Tiflis: Izdatelskaia komissiia Kraevogo Soveta Kavkazskoi Armii, 1917. Pamphlet, apparently published in late spring or early summer.

Voitinskii, Vladimir S. Gody pobed i porazhenii. 2 vols. Berlin, St. Petersburg, and Moscow: I. I. Grzhebina, 1923–24. See also Woytinsky.

———. K chemu stremitsia koalitsionnoe pravitelstvo. Petrograd: Kniga, 1917. This was evidently published early in the coalition period.

———. Krestianin, rabochii i soldat. Petrograd: "Kniga," 1917.

———. Manuscript memoir of 1917, intended as the third volume of his Gody pobed i porazhenii, Nicolaevsky Collection, Hoover Institution, Stanford, Calif.

Volobuev, P. V., ed. "Iz istorii borby Vremennogo pravitelstva s revoliutsiei," Istoricheskii Arkhiv, 1960, No. 5, 78–86.

———. Proletariat i burzhuaziia Rossii v 1917. Moskva: Mysl, 1964.

Von Laue, Theodore. "Westernization, Revolution and the Search for a Basis of Authority—Russia in 1917," Soviet Studies, XIX, 2 (October 1967), 156–80.

———. Why Lenin? Why Stalin? A Reappraisal of the Russian Revolution, 1900–1930. Philadelphia: Lippincott, 1964.

Voronovich, N. "Zapiski predsedatelia soveta soldatskikh deputatov," Arkhiv grazhdenskoi voiny, II (1922), 7–102.

Wade, Rex A. "Argonauts of Peace: The Soviet Delegation to Western Europe in the Summer of 1917," Slavic Review, XXVI, 3 (September 1967), 453–67.

———. "Irakli Tsereteli and Siberian Zimmerwaldism," Journal of Modern History, XXXIX, 4 (December 1967), 425–31.

Warth, Robert D. The Allies and the Russian Revolution: From the Fall of the Monarchy to the Peace of Brest-Litovsk. Durham, N.C.: Duke University Press, 1954.

White, James D. "The Kornilov Affair: A Study in Counter-Revolution," Soviet Studies, XX, 2 (October 1968), 187–205.

Winship, North. U.S. Consulate Reports: Reports of Consul North Winship at Petrograd to Secretary of State, March 20–July 10, 1917. Hoover Institution, Stanford, Calif.

Woytinsky, W. S. [V. S. Voitinskii]. Stormy Passage: A Personal History Through Two Russian Revolutions to Democracy and Freedom: 1905–1960. New York: Vanguard Press, 1961.

Zeman, Z. A. B., ed. Germany and the Revolution in Russia: Documents of the German Foreign Ministry. London: Oxford University Press, 1958.

Zenzinov, V. M. Collection of manuscripts, incorporating the V. M. Chernov collection of manuscripts. Russian and East European Archive, Columbia University.

――――. "Fevralskie dni," *Novyi Zhurnal*, XXXIV (1953), 188–211; XXXV (1953), 208–40.

――――. Iz zhizni revoliutsionera. Paris: n.p., 1919.

――――. "Zlodeianie; pamiati Abrama Rafailovicha Gotsa," *Za Svobodu*, No. 18 (July 1947), 124–30.

Zhordania, Noi N. Moia Zhizn. Stanford, Calif.: Hoover Institution Press, 1968.

"Zhurnal soedinennago zasedaniia komissii po oborone i po inostrannym delam," *Byloe*, 1918, No. 6, 28–41.

Zinoviev, G. E. Sochineniia. Vol. VII (2 parts). Leningrad: Gosizdat, 1925.